From Exile
to Redemption

The Fiction of Isaac Bashevis Singer

Grace Farrell Lee

SOUTHERN ILLINOIS UNIVERSITY PRESS
Carbondale and Edwardsville

Library of Congress Cataloging-in-Publication Data

Farrell Lee, Grace.
From exile to redemption.

Bibliography: p.
Includes index.
1. Singer, Isaac Bashevis, 1904–   —
Criticism and interpretation.   I. Title.
PJ5129.S49Z65   1987   839′.0933   86–20302
ISBN O-8093-1330-8

For Matthew and Elizabeth

God *is* that all things are possible,
and that all things are possible *is* God.

—Kierkegaard
The Sickness unto Death

Contents

Acknowledgments

I am indebted to Professors Lois A. Cuddy, Nicole X. Cauvin, Mariann Russell, and Joseph Grau, who read parts of the manuscript; to Professor David H. Hirsch, who read my interpretations of English texts against the Yiddish texts; and especially to Professor Robin McAllister, for his generosity and critical acumen in commenting upon each draft of each chapter of the book.

Thanks go to my husband, Lawrence Lee, and to the many students who have shared my enthusiasm for Singer's work and encouraged me in so many ways to complete this book, particularly Marge Bernardo, Pat Braun, Bonnie Evans, Ruth Fine, Shirley Fish, Ruth Green, Mary Ann Hyde, Florence Saunders, and Eileen Zurich.

I thank Frank Sullivan, James and Carol Walker, Josie Porto, and Lynne Roberts for helping to make life smoother during many months of writing, Carol Vaniotis for typing the manuscript, and Lawrence Lee and Michelle Louis for proofreading.

Finally, I would like to acknowledge the generous support of the National Endowment for the Humanities, which provided me with a fellowship for a year during which much of this book was written. Yale, Harvard, and Brown universities provided research facilities, and my university's grant program supplied funding for some research and typing costs.

Portions of this book appeared in slightly different form in the following publications: "Isaac Bashevis Singer: Mediating between the Biblical and the Modern," *Modern Language Studies* 15 (Fall 1985): 117–23; "'Gimpel the Fool': The Kabbalic Basis of Singer's Secular Vision," *Essays in Literature* 13 (Spring 1986): 157–66; "The Hidden God of Isaac Bashevis Singer," *The Hollins Critic* 10 (December 1973). Reprinted by permission.

From Exile to Redemption

1   *Analogues of Exile*

A Hidden God and an Empty Cosmos

Isaac Bashevis Singer's short story "Old Love" concludes as
Harry Bendiner, eighty-two year old millionaire, survivor of
three wives and two children, dreams of meditating in a solitary British Columbian tent with the daughter of a dead love
"on why a man is born and why he must die" (*Passions* 42).
In one way or another, each of Singer's stories is a variation
on this essential meditation, and the exiled meditant is the
prototypical Singer character. The questions posed by the
meditant and the exile he endures are intimately connected,
for while the questions concern a search for a source of meaning which might give significance to human life and which
might explain the mystery of mortality, the exile can be defined as the separation of humankind from that source of
meaning. Ultimately, to find answers to one's questions is to
be redeemed from one's exile.

In *The Myth of Sisyphus*, Camus defined that modern phenomenon, absurdity, in terms of exile. He tells us that we confront our exile in a universe which does not yield up answers
to our question of "why?" He writes:

> A world that can be explained even with bad reasons is a familiar
> world. But, on the other hand, in a universe suddenly divested of
> illusions and lights, man feels an alien, a stranger. His exile is
> without remedy since he is deprived of the memory of a lost
> home or the hope of a promised land. This divorce between man
> and his life, the actor and his setting, is properly the feeling of
> absurdity. ("Absurd Reasoning" 5)

The exiled meditant, deprived of a promised land, while recognizable as an essential figure in Camus and much of modern literature, certainly has its metaphorical echoes in biblical material.

The Book of Job, in particular, with its suggestions that we are "born to wander blindly" (3:23), exiled from any source of ultimate meaning, presages modern depictions of existence.[1] For Job, God "hides his face," leaving humankind to ask:

> But where can wisdom be found?
> And where is the source of understanding?
> No man knows the way to it;
> it is not found in the land of living men. (28:12–13)

 Singer, perhaps more so than any other serious contemporary writer, utilizes biblical images to confront such questions of meaning. In so doing, his fiction secularizes religious material, making analogous the biblical image of a God who hides his face and the modern image of a cosmos empty of transcendent meaning.

This is a dangerous analogue, for the specter of God would seem to cancel the profound cosmic emptiness which is the essence of the modern vision. But an absent God who hides his face provides metaphoric ambivalences which Singer uses to enrich, with a bit of uncertainty, the dogmatic starkness of the contemporary view. It is dangerous in yet another way, for a fundamentalist reading of Singer can lead to the all too easy dismissal of him as other than modern, a criticism which he has learned to ignore, but which I would rather put into a new perspective. For, although their cries are couched in religious terms, as his characters incessantly search out their elusive God, Singer evokes a universe akin to that of modern secular absurdists, a place where humankind appears to be exiled from any source of meaning and where the phenomenal world forever disintegrates about us.

While Camus' modern man bewails a universe which remains silent in the face of human questioning, in a parallel image, Singer's characters call out to a God who perpetually recedes from their grasp. Job shakes his fist towards a hidden God, crying, "If only I knew how to find him" (23:3), and Singer creates a cacophony of voices shouting to the universe, each posing questions in its own human way. As a child, Asa Heshel Bannet asks: "How high is the sky? How deep is the earth? What's at the other side of the end of the world? Who made God?" (*Moskat* 26). Later, in the face of his wife's death, he asks: "'Hadassah, where are you now? Do you know? Do you exist?' Was it possible that past time had no being? Was there nothing but the momentary present?" (607). "How is it possible, after all," grieves Haiml Chentshimer in *Shosha*, "that someone should simply vanish? How can someone who lived, loved, hoped, and wrangled with God and with himself just disappear?" (269). And, as Harry Bendiner asks, for what were we born and why must we die?

Like the townspeople of Krasnobród who ponder and explain yet never discover the truth, "because if there is such a thing as truth it is as intricate and hidden as a crown of feathers" ("A Crown of Feathers," *Crown* 30), so Singer's characters speculate—humorously, morosely, endlessly. In *Enemies, A Love Story*, Herman Broder suggests in despair, "Wasn't it possible that a Hitler presided on high and inflicted suffering on imprisoned souls?" (53). Or perhaps, a dybbuk whispers to Morris Feitelzohn in *Shosha:* "God suffers from a kind of divine amnesia that made Him lose the purpose of His creation. . . . God tried to do too much in too short an eternity. He has lost both criterion and control and is badly in need of help. . . . I see Him as a very sick God, so bewildered by His galaxies and the multitude of laws He established that He doesn't know what He aimed for to start with" (34).

Sometimes it seems that the only truth is that with which the narrator concludes "Neighbors": "The radiator near which I sat hissed and hummed: 'Dust, dust, dust.' The singsong penetrated my bones together with the warmth. It repeated a truth as old as the world, as profound as sleep" (*Crown* 320).

Singer's novel *Shosha* ends as two friends, exiled in Tel Aviv after the Holocaust, sit in a darkening room, waiting, as one says with a laugh, for an answer. Their final conversation expresses feelings of abandonment and resentment in a world devoid of revelation. Haiml says:

> "If God is wisdom, how can there be foolishness? And if God is life, how can there be death? I lie at night, a little man, a half-squashed fly, and I talk with the dead, with the living, with God—if He exists—and with Satan, who certainly does exist. I ask them, 'What need was there for all this?' and I wait for an answer. What do you think, Tsutsik, is there an answer somewhere or not?"
>
> "No, no answer."
>
> "Why not?"
>
> "There can't be any answer for suffering—not for the sufferer."
>
> "In that case, what am I waiting for?"
>
> Genia opened the door. "Why are you two sitting in the dark, eh?"
>
> Haiml laughed. "We're waiting for an answer." (277)

Singer here speaks of humankind as Isaiah spoke of the Children of Israel: "We wait for light, but behold obscurity; for brightness, but we walk in darkness. We grope for the wall like the blind, and we grope as if we had no eyes: we stumble at noon day as in the night, we are in desolate places as dead men" (59:9–10). With its Beckett-like despair of waiting, the ending of *Shosha* becomes an image of the modern condition. Darkness spreads throughout the room as it spreads throughout Singer's stories and his universe; yet, as *Shosha* ends, the two men still sit in the midst of the darkness waiting in exile for an answer, an answer which they fear will never come. Yet still they wait.

Singer creates fiction which has the power to make us know that we all wait. We wait in exile for an answer, or, like Gimpel the Fool, we wait for the true world where even Gimpel will not be deceived and where revelation will be more than a faint glimmer in a darkened room.

Harry Bendiner of "Old Love" waits in his plastic chaise, on his balcony, eleven stories up from Miami Beach, brooding in solitude on how he is "condemned to live alone and to die alone" (*Passions* 27). The Angel of Death had taken his family from him, but Harry, as suspicious as he is rich, completes the process which death began by exiling himself from any but the most casual of human contacts. Through a series of paltry fantasies, he experiences the world as hostile and threatening: "Maybe someone was following him. Maybe some crook had found out how rich he was and was scheming to kidnap him. Although the day was bright and the street full of people, no one would interfere if he was grabbed, forced into a car, and dragged off to some ruin or cave. No one would pay ransom for him" (30). Harry's fears are so insistent, and for the most part so unfounded, that they create an edge of amusement which serves to exile even the reader from this lonely old man whose paranoia is tinged with self-pity.

His whining fears are symptomatic of a profound struggle within himself. As each of his days takes on a shape like all the others—breakfast, elevator, mail, checks, stock exchange office or bank, nap, dinner—Harry's routine is punctuated by a single, simple question: "Why go on living?" This question, always threatening to break through the surface of his life, becomes the center of the story.

Camus' absurd man finds many echoes in the aged Harry Bendiner. Camus tells us that the "stage set" which is the fragile surface of our lives can collapse suddenly when the question "why?" emerges. Like Harry Bendiner, Camus' everyman moves through his day:

> Rising, streetcar, four hours in the office or the factory, meal, streetcar, four hours of work, meal, sleep, and Monday Tuesday Wednesday Thursday Friday and Saturday according to the same rhythm—this path is easily followed most of the time. But one day the "why" arises and everything begins in that weariness tinged with amazement. "Begins"—this is important. Weariness comes at the end of the acts of a mechanical life, but at the same time it inaugurates the impulse of consciousness. It awakens consciousness and provokes what follows. (10)

What follows is our recognition of the irrationality of the world, of the strangeness of the world. That which was once familiar is now alien and distant. We begin to feel the separateness of our reality from that of all others. We begin to confront our exile in an absurd universe.

Job, too, reduced to a leprous beast, stripped of children and property, no longer certain of his connection with anything beyond the limits of his own mortality, he too, like Camus' absurd man, is finally forced out of a life which provided him with comfortable answers and into a confrontation with the ambiguities of human existence.[2]

"What is man," Job asks, "that thou makest much of him / and turnest thy thoughts toward him, / only to punish him morning by morning / or to test him every hour of the day?" (7:17–18). This cry of anguish, "What is man?," was once an easily answered question. Personally, Job was a good and upright man; socially, he had status as a successful property owner and father; metaphysically, he was in close dialogue with his God. Such complacent, rather superficial answers are ready-made by social and religious structures for Job, for Harry Bendiner, and for everyone who does not wish to look deeply into the ultimate questions and to face the awesomeness and the terrors which lie beneath the surfaces of reality.

Such a confrontation is one which Harry Bendiner would rather avoid; "one couldn't constantly brood about the fact that everything was vanity of vanities. It was easier to think about practical matters" (25–26). The practical, commercial world of Miami, thickly peopled with those who ask "to buy or not to buy," reveals, in this playfully obvious allusion to *Hamlet*, the essence of human questioning. "Man is no more than a puff of wind, / his days a passing shadow," says the Psalmist (144:4); "a foul and pestilent congregation of vapors" if oftentimes seems to Hamlet (II.ii.314). Singer literalizes Shakespeare's disease metaphors, and for Harry Bendiner, the questions of philosophy are outshouted by the complaints of an aged body; the functioning of his bowels becomes more important than the workings of the universe. For Hamlet, Denmark is a prison, and he could count himself king of infinite space though surrounded by a nutshell, if he had not bad dreams. But Harry Bendiner is imprisoned within his apartment, isolated from all those around him, fearful of the world outside, and he cannot remember his dreams: they "dissolved like foam" (25). Harry is exiled from that deep dream world of his own self.

It is the chance encounter with love—for an elderly neighbor, Ethel, who soon throws herself to her death from a window—which wrenches Harry from his immersion in the materialism of the world to face the questions which lie in wait for every human being. Ethel's friendship makes him realize how lonely he has been and how empty is his world. Separated from her by only the thin walls of their apartments, Harry finally acknowledges that "walls possessed a power of their own" (38).

Harry Bendiner comes to a point where the questions break through the surface of his life, and he wants to direct the rest of his days to them. Although we leave him just as he was when first sighted, sitting in his plastic chaise on his balcony eleven stories up from Miami Beach, he has been transformed. Where once he brooded upon his personal exile, Harry has come to recognize a larger exile, one which, paradoxically, can be shared and, thus, in the very act of that sharing, overcome.

Job is also forced from his complacency to find the path which is his existence walled up. Harry had felt the thin walls of his apartment assume a power of their own, and in "An Absurd Reasoning," Camus reminds us of the nature of walls. They are the limitations of our existence, limitations which culminate in death, limitations which we long to transcend in some meaningful way.[3] Job is forced to acknowledge his mortal limitations and his longing to transcend them. But the resentment Job feels towards his God renders him incapable of the prayer dialogue which once was the sustenance of his life. He feels abandoned by a God who has retreated from him, who has "hidden his face," and who can no longer be found. Job is in exile from his God.

The absence of God from Job's world is the spiritual equi-

valent of the secular dilemma defined by Camus. Absurdity,
Camus tells us, is the quester's confrontation with a universe
which does not give forth an answer, which remains silent in
the face of human questioning. This silent universe is the
same as that confronted by Job and by each of Singer's characters: by Tsutsik and Haiml Chentshiner as they wait in their
darkening room, by Asa Bannet as he laments the death of his
wife, by Harry Bendiner as he lies belching and hiccupping
on his bed, unable to comprehend the suicide of his newfound
love, unable to know day from dream, unable anymore to perform those rituals of his mechanical life:

> Well, from now on I won't hope for anything, he decided with the
> solemnity of a man taking an oath. He felt cold, and he covered
> himself with the blanket.
>   It was ten past eight in the morning when he came out of his
> daze. A dream? No, the letter lay on the table. That day Harry
> Bendiner did not go down for his mail. He did not prepare break-
> fast for himself, nor did he bother to bathe and dress. He kept on
> dozing on the plastic chaise on the balcony and thinking about
> that other Sylvia—Ethel's daughter—who was living in a tent in
> British Columbia. Why had she run away so far? he asked him-
> self. Did her father's death drive her into despair? Could she not
> stand her mother? Or did she already at her age realize the
> futility of all human efforts and decide to become a hermit? Is she
> endeavoring to discover herself, or God? An adventurous idea
> came into the old man's mind: to fly to British Columbia, find the
> young woman in the wilderness, comfort her, be a father to her,
> and perhaps try to meditate together with her on why a man is
> born and why he must die. (41–42)

While the silent universe of which Camus speaks is not necessarily a God-filled universe, the feelings of abandonment and
resentment and alienation exist whether one looks up to the
heavens and shakes a fist at an absent God or whether one
sees an empty cosmos which does not provide answers to one's
questions. These are different contexts in which to express
the same human predicament: Harry Bendiner, Camus' everyman, and Job are alienated from a source of ultimate meaning.

They cry out and there is no response to their anguish. They are each alone in a silent universe.

Of course, the crucial difference between the secular and the biblical models lies in the perspective each holds for the possibility of finding or receiving answers to the ultimate questions. Camus says that our "wild longing for clarity," our human need for an answer to the question "why," confronts again and again "the unreasonable silence of the world" (21). Harry Bendiner confronts the silence and in so doing finds the questions towards which he dreams of directing his life. Job confronts the silence, but ultimately it is broken by the voice of a God who speaks from a whirlwind. Job again moves into dialogue with his God. However, the nature of God's response to Job does not touch upon the essence of his questioning. He is returned to the very condition which once had blinded him to the awesome questions about human existence. As Singer says: "At the end Job is rewarded. He has more beautiful daughters and more donkeys and so on and so on, but we feel that this is not an answer to Job's suffering" (Farrell Lee, "Seeing and Blindness" 156–57).

Even this renewed dialogue between humankind and the universe, however flawed, is not reached in modern literature. Instead, the silence continues; the abandonment deepens. Singer, in making metaphorical use of the image of God's removal of himself from the universe, expresses Camus' "wild longing for clarity" and our inability to find it, our feelings of abandonment and of exile. That God is hidden means that our source of meaning, that which can provide answers to our questions of "why?", that which can give significance to us beyond the mortal limitations of our lives, cannot be found.

Moses Maimonides, in the twelfth-century *Guide of the Perplexed*, discusses many aspects of God's hiddenness which Singer plays upon in his fiction.[4] To see the face of God, Maimonides explains, indicates an apprehension of the nature of God, a knowledge which is "inaccessible in its very nature. . . . *But My face shall not be seen* [means] that the true reality of My existence as it veritably is cannot be grasped" (49,

86). If we can think of God as the metaphor for a source of ultimate meaning, then this biblical image of God's hidden face can express for us the secular perspective that in its very nature ultimate meaning is inaccessible.[5] The "wild longing for clarity whose call," Camus says, "echoes in the human heart" (16) can never be satisfied. The universe is incomprehensible. To see the face of God is a metaphor expressing the acquisition of ultimate knowledge. And the image of God's hiddenness is the correlative of the silence of the universe in the face of the human need to know. The human predicament, then, is both irresolvable and absurd, for the silence is irrevocable and it defies the questioning nature of humankind.

Moreover, to have the face of God hidden also indicates, Maimonides says, "a privation of providence [which] leaves one abandoned and a target to all that may happen and come about. . . . And just as the withdrawal of providence is referred to as the *hiding of the face*—as in its dictum: *As for Me, I will surely hide My face*—it also is referred to as *going*, which has the meaning to turn away from a thing. Thus Scripture says: *I will go and return to My place*" (54). The hiding of God's face, then, is also an expression of the emotional dilemma humankind faces—alone, separate, exiled. And the withdrawal of God from the universe expresses the abandonment humankind feels, lost in a universe which is intractable in the face of the human need for significance.

Maimonides also explains that to see God's face is to speak to God, to be in dialogue with God, "as a presence to another presence without an intermediary. . . . *Face* is also an adverb of place that is rendered in Arabic by the words: 'in front of thee' or 'in thy presence'" (86). To have the face of God hidden is the ultimate expression of exile—to not be there, or to have that place of meaning removed from where one is.

Thus, in Singer's hands, the hidden face of God becomes a central image of intricate complexity. The inaccessibility of God, his facelessness, his silence, his exile from humankind, and humankind's exile from him create the symbolic context of

Singer's fiction. But while his work draws upon religious images, its significance is not limited to a religious context. The religious material functions as an overall symbol system which enables Singer to explore the complexities of the human condition and to confront not only the traditional problems of faith and doubt, the existence of evil and the inexplicable mystery of creation, but also those typically modern concerns of alienation, which is exile, and absurdity, which is silence.

The balance which Singer maintains between the biblical and the secular is an uneasy one. He uses biblical material metaphorically in a way which deepens our understanding of what has come to be seen as the modern dilemma. But inherent in the biblical material, no matter the context in which it is used, is hope—hope that the exile may be eased, hope that the silence may be breached, hope that our disbelief may prove to be unnecessary. It is this which distinguishes Singer from his contemporaries, this quality of hope, this belief that no matter how dark the night, we ought to sit and wait, for anything is possible.

2   *Belief and Disbelief*

The Kabbalic Basis of Singer's Secular Vision

"Gimpel the Fool" concludes as Singer's most famous of lonely wanderers lies in a hovel by the graveyard, shrouds prepared in his beggar's sack. More palpable than the worms which, Gimpel says, are hungry and the grave which awaits him is his longing for the transcendence which has eluded him all his long life: "No doubt the world is entirely an imaginary world, but it is only once removed from the true world. . . . God be praised: there even Gimpel cannot be deceived" (*Gimpel* 21).

This longing for some ultimate clarity, beyond deception, and an inability to find it, define Gimpel's exile in a universe which remains silent in the face of human questioning. Although the mere mention of "God" in Gimpel's final words seems to affirm a traditional religious transcendence, a closer look at Singer's handling of his sources of inspiration reveals that only through his focus on certain aspects of the traditional image of God does he create a secular vision of exile and silence. Singer uses the religious thought of the ancient Kabbalah to explore the godless vision of the modern world, and in so doing, he maintains in his fiction a precarious balance between the biblical and the secular, between belief and disbelief.[1]

The Kabbalah, which simply means "tradition," is a collective term used for a variety of esoteric teachings based on the Torah and developed for generations by Jewish mystics.[2] One of the concerns central to the Kabbalah is the nature of God's presence in creation. The *Zohar*, which is the major Kabbalic text, consisting of several volumes of homilies, commentaries, and expositions on the Torah, refers to God as *Ein-Sof*, an inaccessible, unknowable infinite whose existence it is possible to deduce only through the existence of creation.[3] This hidden God manifests itself in creation by means of ten *sefirot*, which are referred to as attributes of *Ein-Sof*, or its epithets. *Ein-Sof's* calling forth of its *sefirot* in the process of creating the world is conceived of as a revelation of its hidden being or as the articulation of its hidden essence into divine speech (Scholem, *Kabbalah* 99).

However, that version of the *Zohar* which became the pre-eminent text for the culture of Singer's childhood, Polish Hasidism, emphasized not the presence of *Ein-Sof* in the world but rather its exile from the world. This text was developed in the sixteenth century by Rabbi Isaac Luria, one of a small group of religious thinkers in Safed, a Palestinian village. The Safed group, profoundly influenced by the catastrophic expulsion of the Jews from Spain a generation earlier, in 1492, refined the Kabbalah in crucial ways. They interwove the historical experience of the exile of the Jewish people with a mystical understanding of the divine universe, so that at the heart of the Kabbalah "lay a great image of rebirth, the myth of exile and redemption" (Scholem, *On the Kabbalah* 2).[4]

The Lurianic Kabbalah reveals exile to be the condition of the universe and even of God. Luria describes creation not as the progressive manifestation of *Ein-Sof* through emanations but rather as a twofold act, the first of which creates a chasm between God and the world. In Lurianic doctrine, *Ein-Sof* was not revealed in the initial act of creation, but rather was concealed so that the world could be revealed. Only then did *Ein-Sof* create the world through emanations. The first action in creation, called *tzimtzum*, or contraction, is given great emphasis by Luria, becoming a metaphor of divine exile.[5] Simply put, God filled all space and had to contract inward to make a place for creation; or, as it is variously explained, God's radiance filled all space, so that the light had to be dimmed to make a place for creation.

The second stage of the Lurianic creation myth extends the idea of God's exile from the world. After removing itself from the place of creation, *Ein-Sof* began the process of emanation, sending the *sefirot*, sometimes imagined as rays of divine light, into the space provided for creation. Through the *sefirot*, *Ein-Sof* created the cosmos and everything in it. During the process of emanation, the Kabbalists tell us, the *sefirot* entered vessels in order to take form, but the vessels could not contain the light and therefore broke. The divine light was scattered throughout creation. Nothing is where it should be. All being is in exile.

In a sense, God, too, through the *sefirot*, was dispersed throughout the world. Luria, countering the pantheistic implications of the doctrine of emanation, posited a curtain or wall between the world of divinity and the world of creation. The curtain refracts the divine substance back into itself, while it allows a radiance to filter through. Thus, "not *En-Sof* itself is dispersed in the nether worlds, but only a radiance" (Scholem, *Major Trends* 273). Luria's clarification serves to underscore once more the exile and inaccessibility of God. Creation is God's cosmic exile. Paradoxically, God is both nowhere and yet his radiance is everywhere dispersed. Thus, throughout their lives Singer's characters have intimations of transcendence, fleeting moments of clarity when they seem to have touched upon a larger truth, but these moments can never be sustained; they are "as intricate and hidden as a crown of feathers" ("A Crown of Feathers," *Crown* 30).

The implied, yet inaccessible, God of the Kabbalists becomes, in Singer's hands, a hidden and perhaps altogether absent God whose very existence is open to question. Out of the ancient religious tradition to which he is heir, Singer forms a modern, secular vision. He shifts the emphasis of the Kabbalic creation story, transforming the *Zohar* from a system of belief into a prescription for doubt. His work accentuates the startlingly modern implications of the Lurianic images of the exile of God in the first stage of creation, implications which suggest that the very existence of the world is predicated upon the absence of God from it. As a soul in the first sphere of heaven remarks: "'He is supposed to dwell in the seventh heaven, which is an infinity away. One thing we can be sure of, He's not here'" ("The Warehouse," *Seance* 129). Or, as elsewhere, a character says in despair: "Before Ain Sof created the world He first dimmed His light and formed a void. It was only in this void that the Emanation commenced. This divine absence may be the very essence of creation" (*Shosha* 51).

In Singer's work, the God we find is one who has created a world devoid of the possibility of God. We are teased with hints of transcendence only to be reminded that the world exists in the absence of any such transcendence. The mere mention of "God" in a Singer story, then, serves not to affirm a traditional religious transcendence, as it is so often presumed to do, but rather to suggest cosmic exile, inscrutability, concealment, and silence; it evokes a universe which remains a riddle, a teasing puzzle which we long to comprehend but never can.

In its paradoxical vision of God as both present in and absent from creation, the *Zohar* simultaneously offers possibilities for both belief and disbelief. In "Gimpel the Fool," Singer holds these possibilities in a precarious balance.[6] Gimpel, a believer who extends his willingness to believe to every aspect of his life, is tempted to disbelieve the stories told to him, to deny his faith, and to enact revenge against those who humiliate him for his gullibility. Gimpel builds his life upon belief. "Belief in itself is beneficial," a rabbi tells Gimpel. "It is written that a good man lives by his faith" (17). Extending that faith to all of creation, Gimpel ignores evidence to the contrary and chooses to believe in whatever he is told, that his parents are raised from the dead, that his pregnant fiancée is a virgin, that her children are his own, that the man jumping out of his wife's bed is a figment of his own imagination: "I resolved that I would always believe what I was told. What's the good of *not* believing? Today it's your wife you don't believe; tomorrow it's God Himself you won't take stock in" (13–14).

Gimpel's resolution is difficult to maintain because, even while choosing to believe, he knows that he is deceived. At the end of the story, when he dreams of a truer world, where "even Gimpel cannot be deceived," the believer's pose is undercut by his very words which imply that, indeed, he has been deceived. Earlier, when told that his parents "have stood up from the grave," Gimpel says: "To tell the truth, I knew very well that nothing of the sort had happened, but all the same, as folks were talking, I threw on my wool vest and went out. Maybe something had happened. What did I stand to lose by looking?" (5). At another point, he decides not to defend himself against the humiliating jokesters who play upon him: "I had to believe when the whole town came down on me! . . . What was I to do? I believed them, and I hope at least that did them some good" (4).

Indeed, it does do them some good because Gimpel becomes for the townspeople of Frampol an image of immutable trust in a world devoid of absolute truths, a world from which, as the *Zohar* relates, God has retreated. When he succumbs to temptation and betrays that trust, his dead wife, Elka, returns to him in a vision and cries out, "Because I was false is everything false too?" (19). Her lament expresses the town's need to have Gimpel be true to his unending willingness to believe.[7]

We readers know that the stories Gimpel is told are false. Our disbelief is necessary here, for if we thought the stories to be true, the significance of Gimpel's suspension of disbelief and the scope of his act of faith would be lost to us. The story, then, which we have entered by suspending our disbelief, contains a series of inner stories which necessitate our disbelief and force us to be unlike Gimpel, who is able to extend his belief to encompass everything. We are cast in the role of the disbeliever, for clearly there are necessary limits placed upon our belief.

However, the scope of these limits remains unclear; the ultimate story within the story, which becomes pivotal in the test of Gimpel's faith, is that of the existence of God. Are we to believe or to disbelieve this story? In bringing readers to the point of confronting this question, Singer's story, maintaining its balance between belief and disbelief, places us in the same position of temptation as that in which Gimpel finds himself. What began as a series of decisions typically made by a reader of any fiction—is this or that believable or not?—becomes a problem of faith.

Thus, through his narrative strategy, Singer transforms this simple tale of temptation, into a sophisticated dialectic in which, while Gimpel moves steadfastly in the path of faith, the reader is pushed along a counterpath of skepticism and disbelief until the paths cross and both character and reader must face the central question of faith. Neither the paradoxes of faith in the *Zohar* nor the crisis of faith in "Gimpel" are ever resolved. Singer brings his reader to an unresolved crisis of faith in order to define the human being as one who is confronted by the question of ultimate meaning as a baffling problem and as one who is in exile from any resolution to that problem.

I have said that we enter this story initially by suspending our disbelief, but even this suspension is tentative because the tale is told by one who is thought to be a fool. The opening lines immediately introduce this narrative problem: "I am Gimpel the Fool. I don't think myself a fool. On the contrary. But that's what folks call me" (3). Is he or he is not a fool? To answer this question is essential to the interpretative process as well as to the problem of faith which is implicitly posed by the narrative, that is, is it foolish to believe? By the end of the story, Gimpel posits himself not as a fool but, "on the contrary," as a rather wise old wanderer who makes a firm statement of belief in a transcendent world. "Whatever may be there, it will be real, without complication, without ridicule, without deception. God be praised: there even Gimpel cannot be deceived" (21).

In deciding whether Gimpel is reliable in his storytelling, readers are again involved in a problem of faith, choosing to believe or to disbelieve in the seriousness of Gimpel's statement of transcendence. If we choose to regard Gimpel as unreliable because he is a gullible fool, the final statement of faith is undercut with a biting irony, and we are left to conclude that belief is indeed foolishness. But if we choose to see Gimpel as a wise man, we may be led to conclude that Singer means for us to receive as prophetic the final statement of transcendence.

Variously, Gimpel may be seen as a person who chooses to believe although aware that he is regarded by most as a fool and aware also that his experience in the world always points towards disbelief. This last position helps to solve the question of Gimpel's reliability while leaving the question of the truth of his faith unanswered, i.e., it characterizes him as less naive than he may at first appear to be but perhaps no less foolish in his final choice to believe than he has always seemed. It is also in keeping with the narrative strategies of this particular story which, from its beginning, emphasize the ambiguity of the narrative voice and which, almost throughout, necessitate the reader's skepticism and disbelief. It is only at the point of ultimate temptation, questioning the existence of God, that the story brings us to the inevitability of neither belief nor disbelief. Like the *Zohar,* which offers both possibilities at once, Singer holds the alternatives in equal balance. We only know the choice which Gimpel made—but then Gimpel may be a fool.

The question of Gimpel's foolishness hinges on the discrepancy between what his experiences of the world seem to tell him about that world and what he chooses to believe. Rather than resolving this discrepancy, the story concludes with a most Kabbalic, as well as a most modern, suggestion—that the empirical world itself may be insubstantial. "No doubt the world is entirely an imaginary world . . ." To believe in only it may be the ultimate foolishness.

It is to another significant work of the Kabbalah, the *Sefer*

Yezirah, that we may turn for a fuller understanding of this often puzzling conclusion to "Gimpel the Fool." This brief book of the Kabbalah emphasizes the image of the creator God as primal writer, an image important to all of Kabbalic thought. While the *Zohar* imagined the emanation of the *sefirot* as *Ein-Sof's* articulation of divine attributes into speech, the initial sentence of the *Sefer Yezirah* declares, "In thirty-two mysterious paths of wisdom [consisting of the twenty-two Hebrew letters and the ten *sefirot*] did the Lord write" (Stenring 21).[8] Scholem makes clear that "in the continuous act of the language of creation the godhead is the only infinite speaker, but at the same time he is the original archetypal writer, who impresses his word deep into his created works" ("Name of God" 168).

The universe, therefore, is essentially linguistic, composed by the writer-God out of endless permutations of the Hebrew alphabet. As Scholem puts it: "Every existing thing somehow contains these linguistic elements and exists by their power, whose foundation is one name, i.e., the Tetragrammaton, or, perhaps, the alphabetical order which in its entirety is considered one mystical name. The world-process is essentially a linguistic one, based on the unlimited combinations of the letters" (*Kabbalah* 25). Language, then, infinite in its possibilities, is sacred. At its foundation lies the unnameable name of God, which, if known, would reveal the essence of *Ein-Sof*. Thus, within the hidden recesses of language lies the possibility of ultimate knowledge, truth, meaning. Language, too, constitutes both the action by which the world is created and the matter from which it is created. The act of creation is *Ein-Sof's* articulation of its essence into divine speech, and what is articulated are words and letters. Language, thus, creates reality, and language is reality.

In Hasidic culture, the murmuring of words in prayer is considered in and of itself a holy action because uttering the word constitutes an imitation of God's creative act, while fiction is considered to be a blasphemous use of the sacred word, which should be used only to explicate holy texts or to

tell the tales of holy people. But Singer, exploiting the implications of the *Sefer Yezirah*'s image of God as writer, reveals storytelling to be as much an imitation of the primal
creative act as is prayer and fiction to be as much a source of
truth as is faith. Gimpel's faith is presented in terms of fiction;
it is actualized in his willingness to believe what he is told. If
God is the primal storyteller, then belief is belief in stories,
and the true person of faith is the ideal reader. Thus, willingly
suspending his disbelief, Gimpel makes a fictive necessity
into a mode of life.

Although rendered in archaic diction and oftentimes associated with astrology and magic, particularly with the magical
power of letters and words, the linguistic theory of the Kabbalah is surprisingly modern in its implications.[9] The idea that
language creates reality, that existence may be a dream or a
text, and that we may be mere characters within that text is a
theme which not only Singer but Borges, Nabokov, Fowles,
Coover, Barth, and other modern fiction writers play with repeatedly. It undermines the primacy of empirical reality,
rendering both reality and our own existence tentative, subject
perhaps to the whim of an author's offhand remark. Hasidic
legend holds that before creating the world, God created and
destroyed, like so many rough drafts, seven others (Schaya
107). Truly, as Meir the eunuch reminds us, a word taken back
means obliteration: "What keeps all the world together?" he
asks in "Stories from behind the Stove." "It's all by a word of
the Almighty. If He takes His word back, the whole creation
returns to primeval chaos" (*Kafka* 70–71).

Singer, in imitation of his absent God, fills the void with
fictional worlds, creating and recreating until the universe
becomes a magical collage of new texts, each vying with
God's original for creative primacy. Singer's play with realities
which, although alien to one another, seem to intersect and
thus to call into question their own substantiality, further undermines the assumption that a stable world order, an absolute reality exists. Reality becomes plural and amorphous. We
can slip into one from another like the guest in "A Wedding in

Brownsville" slips inconspicuously from life into death and still attends the wedding. We are often left exiled, like the narrator of "Alone," from our very corporeality: "I was on Collins Avenue in Miami Beach, but I felt like a ghost, cut off from everything. I went into the library and asked a question—the librarian grew frightened. I was like a man who had died, whose space had already been filled" (*Friday* 52). Perhaps, a demon in "Shiddah and Kuziba" suggests, existence is "nothing but a bad dream which God had spun out for a while to distract himself in his eternal night" (*Spinoza* 96). Or, as Gimpel put it, "No doubt the world is entirely an imaginary world."

The potentially revelatory power of the creative word would seem to be rendered mute in the modern world. In "A Friend of Kafka," we are asked: "'Did not God, according to the cabala, create the world by uttering holy words? In the beginning was the Logos.'" But now, this story makes clear, life is reduced to a chess game which we know we cannot win, and language, like that of the women in "Prufrock" who "come and go / Talking of Michelangelo," is diminished to intellectual chitchat: "All talk, talk" (*Kafka* 14, 13).

Such is the language of the stories told by the villagers of Frampol. Theirs is a language devoid of truth, unworthy of belief. Theirs is a language which remains meaningless even as words are uttered, a language through which no transcendence is possible, a language—to use Singer's metaphor—from which God is exiled. Scholem, in his brilliant inquiry, "The Name of God and the Linguistic Theory of the Kabbala," identifies this modern crisis in language:

> What the value and worth of language will be—the language from which God will have withdrawn—is the question which must be posed by those who still believe that they can hear the echo of the vanished word of the creation in the immanence of the world. This is a question to which, in our times, only the poets presumably have the answer. For poets do not share the doubt that most mystics have in regard to language. And poets have one link with the masters of the Kabbala, even when they

reject Kabbalistic theological formulation as being still too emphatic. This link is their belief in language as an absolute, which is as if constantly flung open by dialectics. It is their belief in the mystery of language which has become audible. (194)

It is to literature, then, that we look not only for a depiction of an absurd universe which remains unresponsive to the human need for meaning, but also for the hope, inherent in the Kabbalic conception of language, that through words we may create new sources of meaning. The idealization of language, so prevalent in the sensibilities of modern writers and so ancient in its source, while wreaking much havoc upon empiricism, raises the imagination to sublime heights. If language is sacred, if its hidden essence is truth, then its imaginative acts are preludes to revelation; here again for Singer, faith and fiction converge.

As Singer imitates his absent God, his characters often imitate him, becoming tellers of tales within the tales told about them. It is not a coincidence that Singer's greatest believer, Gimpel the Fool, becomes one of his most notable storytellers, and the story he tells is a tale of faith in the imagination itself.

Even the senseless lies of Frampol are not without significance. In providing Gimpel with an initial focus for his will to believe, these stories eventually help him move towards a deeper faith, a faith in the infinite possibilities of the word. He believes everyone, Gimpel explains early in the story, because "everything is possible, as it is written in the Wisdom of the Fathers, I've forgotten just how" (4).

Gimpel gives no one reality priority, but instead opens himself to all worlds, dreams, apparitions, and tales, to all possibilities of truth. Herein does Gimpel become not only the true man of faith but also the storyteller who conflates his articles of faith with his theories of fiction. In the final four paragraphs of the story, Gimpel draws careful connections between the exiled wanderer who observes the world's plenitude and the storyteller, the dreamer, and the believer, each of whom imagines an infinity of worlds:

I wandered over the land, and good people did not neglect me. After many years I became old and white; I heard a great deal, many lies and falsehoods, but the longer I lived the more I understood that there were really no lies. Whatever doesn't really happen is dreamed at night. It happens to one if it doesn't happen to another, tomorrow if not today, or a century hence if not next year. What difference can it make? . . .

Going from place to place, eating at strange tables, it often happens that I spin yarns—improbable things that could never have happened—about devils, magicians, windmills, and the like. . . .

So it is with dreams too. . . .

No doubt the world is entirely an imaginary world, but it is only once removed from the true world. (20–21)

Singer creates Gimpel in such a way that the character is finally made in the author's own image and likeness, spinning improbable yarns about devils and magicians, defying, with a commitment to the limitless possibilities of the word, the narrow conventions of the "real." Lies and deceptions, dreams and improbable yarns—such is the stuff of fiction as it gropes its way towards truth.

Like the God who is exiled so that the world may be revealed, Gimpel finally exiles himself from Frampol, revealing the vacuity of the town, like the empty cosmos it mirrors. Only then does he reveal to himself the true nature of his faith. In fact, Gimpel was always in exile—from the villagers and from the truth. Only when he concretizes his spiritual exile by becoming an actual wanderer does he finally come, not to a resolution of the contradictions between belief and disbelief, which Singer found in the *Zohar* and which run throughout the story, but to a vision of the truth which can contain all contradictions, a vision suggested by the linguistic theories of the *Sefer Yezirah*, a vision of the truth of storytelling.

Gimpel moves from a belief which is blind, yet riddled with doubt, to an acceptance of the mysterious complexity of the universe, where anything can be true because the possibilities of language, which creates that universe, are infinite. If the Kabbalah is "a great image of rebirth, the myth of exile and redemption" (Scholem, *On the Kabbalah* 2) then, at the end, by the side of the graveyard, Gimpel is reborn, redeemed into a faith to which he can firmly adhere, a faith in the imagination, a faith in the fecundity of fiction.

The vision which Singer provides us offers no ultimate clarity to the paradoxes of the human condition, no prophetic proclamation which might breach the "silence that enfolds us" (Beckett, *The Unnamable*). Instead, it offers the hope which is inherent in the Kabbalic idea of Logos. It offers hope in the creative possibilities of language, language which creates reality and which is reality.

3 Demonic Dimensions of Exile

Reading the Short Stories

Beneath the surface of the simple folktale, "Gimpel the Fool," we have seen an elaborate process wherein the dynamics of fiction are tightly joined with the assumptions of faith. Singer, in the most modern of manners, manipulates fictional conventions to further his thematic considerations and posits a new transcendence based, not upon the supernatural, but upon the infinite possibilities of language and the imagination.

Storytelling itself is a motif which runs throughout the fiction.[1] God, Gimpel, and I. B. Singer are not the only storytellers to fill the silence of the universe with a collage of texts. Singer's fiction overflows with a cacophony of narrative voices—whispering, gossiping, sharing secret stories. In tales with contemporary settings, narrators, in varying degrees rather closely resembling the author himself, are writers of note who share stories with us or are pursued by those obsessed with sharing theirs. Slyly and with great imagination, demonic narrators recite their evil deeds, while pious Gimpels or nameless narrators whisper secret tales, and groups of beggars or scholars in poorhouses and studyhouses sit around sputtering stoves, outdoing one another with their confidences.

For Singer, storytelling is a significant action, rooted in the primal act of creation and associated with the linguistic theories of the Kabbalah. Often he makes playful allusions to these associations. In "The Last Demon," in which a vision of life after the Holocaust reveals a world in which people are so evil that demons are irrelevant, one lonely demon feeds on letters in a Yiddish storybook. Like an overly scholastic rabbi, he "tortuously interpret[s] and reinterpret[s] each dot": "Yes, as long as a single volume remains, I have something to sustain me. As long as the moths have not destroyed the last page, there is something to play with. What will happen when the last letter is no more, I'd rather not bring to my lips" (*Friday* 130).

The tale contains a subtle play on the idea of story as that which has created and which sustains not only this particular demon but the entire universe. The final lines read, "*When the last letter is gone, / The last of the demons is gone*" (*Friday* 130). Quite literally, when the last letter is gone, this story will be over, and thus the demon, the narrator of the story, will be done, i.e., finished with his narration. And when the last letter is gone and the story is over, then the demon, who is also the subject of the story, will be done, i.e., he will no longer exist. And again, "What will happen when the last letter is no more, I'd rather not bring to my lips," for if all of reality is a linguistic construct—a story, a text—then, when the last letter is gone, all of creation will cease to exist. As a dead fiddler tells us, "Reality itself hangs by a thread," and it is a linguistic thread ("The Dead Fiddler," *Seance* 51). Even the dead fiddler, who is a dybbuk inhabiting the body of a young girl, whiles away his time entertaining the village rabble with his storytelling.

Singer creates labyrinths of illusion by layering story upon story, world upon world, until, as a character out of Nabokov once said, you feel "as if you were rising up from stratum to stratum but never reaching the surface, never emerging into reality. . . . Yet who knows? Is this reality, *the* final reality or just a new deceptive dream?" (*King, Queen, Knave*). As Gimpel the Fool speculated, "No doubt the world is entirely an imaginary world, but it is only once removed from the true world."

As if to caution readers who are too eager to reach for the imminence of that "true world," Singer, with a skepticism made comic in a tale like "The Warehouse," humorously portrays the exile of even the inhabitants of heaven from the "true world." The reader is transported to the first sphere of heaven where angels scratch buttocks with wings and naked souls stand about in queues "waiting for the issuance of their new bodies" (*Seance* 125). Amid haggling over mismade bodies and envy towards those in the higher spheres of heaven, there is resentment against a God who is conspicuously absent, who never shows his face. As one agnostic soul stacked up in the warehouse puts it: "'He is supposed to dwell in the seventh heaven, which is an infinity away. One thing we can be sure of, He's not here'" (129). God, that ultimate source of meaning, is always an infinity away, and thus life, rendered as existence in a warehouse, is reduced to a comic and cosmic meaninglessness.

Singer's skepticism, directed towards infinity where the Divine perpetually recedes from the grasp of humankind, reverses upon itself in "Jachid and Jechidah." Set again in heaven, here atheistic souls disbelieve in Earth, producing an eerie perspective on our own incredulity. The pious in heaven believe that when a heavenly soul transgresses and dies, it

immediately began to rot and was soon covered with a slimy stuff called semen. Then a grave digger put it into a womb where it turned into some sort of fungus and was henceforth known as a child. Later on, began the tortures of Gehenna: birth, growth, toil. For according to the morality books, death was not the final stage. Purified, the soul returned to its source. But what evidence was there for such beliefs? So far as Jechidah knew, no one had ever returned from Earth. The enlightened Jechidah believed that the soul rots for a short time and then disintegrates into a darkness of no return. (*Friday* 82–83)

Like many of Singer's stories, "Jachid and Jechidah" calls into question the Kantian foundations of empirical reality; "time and space, cause and effect, number and relation" are the illusions of our anticelestial world which cease only during sleep and dream, during which the sojourn on Earth is seen as "temporary and illusory, a trial and means of purification" (89).[2]

In one manner or another, all of Singer's storytelling, while reaching out for a world of truth, turns around upon itself, making even more immeasurable the labyrinth,[3] making clear both that there is no clarity and that the universe is necessarily incomprehensible. Towards the end of "The Dead Fiddler," as villagers try to sort out the unlikely events of demonic possession, we are told that "Heaven and earth have sworn that the truth shall remain forever hidden" (63). Once again in Singer's fiction, we are reminded that clarity of vision—truth—is, by the very nature of creation, inaccessible to us. Such is the meaning of the hiddenness of God; it is the correlative of the silence of the universe in the face of the human need to know; it is an expression of the most profound human exile—exile from truth, from clarity, from meaning.

Thus, Singer's storytellers conclude their tales not with answers nor with moral allegories nor exempla but with questions or suppositions which serve only to deepen the impenetrable mysteries of creation. "The world is full of puzzles," we read in "Esther Kreindel the Second." "It is possible that not even Elijah will be able to answer all our questions when the Messiah comes. Even God in seventh Heaven may not have solved all the mysteries of His Creation. This may be the reason He conceals His face" (*Friday* 80).

But despite the endlessness of this exile from ultimate meaning, Singer's stories continue to explore the deep recesses of the hidden, often employing, as Gimpel put it, "devils, magicians, windmills, and the like" (*Gimpel* 20). Singer's notion of the transcendent power of the imagination and his conception of language as a creator rather than as a mirror of reality frees his storytelling from the mandates of realism, enabling him to create a multiplicity of worlds, some teeming with fantastical life, each used for endless speculation on the human condition and the nature of creation.

In Singer's universe, a diaphanous net "as soft as a cobweb and as full of holes" ("The Mirror," *Gimpel* 77) is the only partition separating nature from supernature, labyrinth from labyrinth. And within that net hides a host of evil beings.

Whatever its guise, whether devils and dybbuks ever lurking on the periphery of the unseen world or satanic specters of the Nazi Holocaust, the existence of evil sometimes seems to be the one sure fact in the otherwise illusory material world of Singer's fiction. Cunning, murmurous voices of demonic narrators permeate the folktale worlds of the short stories. "I was created," confides one, "half spirit, half demon, half air, half shade, horned like a buck and winged like a bat, with the mind of a scholar and the heart of a highwayman. I am and I am not" ("From the Diary of One Not Born," *Gimpel* 135).

Singer's devils function both as chaotic invaders of the external world, and as specters of the human psyche, rising up out of imagination or of dream. In "The Little Shoemakers," Abba Shuster, bewildered on his first trip outside of Frampol, creates demons from his fear of the unknown: "The train arrived in the middle of the night with a hissing and whistling, a racket and din. Abba took the headlights of the locomotive for the eyes of a hideous devil, and shied away from the funnels with their columns of sparks and smoke and their clouds of steam" (*Gimpel* 102). Or again, Itche Nokhum, semiconscious from too much fasting, conjures up a demonic hallucination:

> Something began to stir in the dark by the door—a coiling wisp of vapor, airy and misty. . . . The specter flowed toward him, dragging its tail of slime like a chick prematurely breaking out of the shell. "The Primeval Substance!" . . . He wanted to speak to the night-creature, but he was robbed of the power of speech. For a time he watched dumbly as she approached, half woman, half shapeless ooze, a monstrous fungus straining to break away from its root, a creature put together in haste. After a while she began to melt away. Pieces dropped from her. The face dissolved, the hair scattered, the nose stretched out and became a snout, as in the manikins that people put on their window sills in winter to mock the frost. ("The Fast," *Friday* 114)

Even in the novels and tales set in Warsaw, New York, or Miami, far from the superstitions of the *shtetl*, ordinary reality continually dissolves into nightmare as devils are conjured up out of shadow and light. "We rode past a pier," the narrator of "Alone," vacationing in Miami, tells us, "where freshly caught fish were being weighed. Their bizarre colors, gory skin wounds, glassy eyes, mouths full of congealed blood, sharp-pointed teeth—all were evidence of a wickedness as deep as the abyss. Men gutted the fishes with an unholy joy. The bus passed a snake farm, a monkey colony. I saw houses eaten up by termites and a pond of brackish water in which the descendants of the primeval snake crawled and slithered" (*Friday* 53).

Perhaps no other facet of Singer's writing so discomforts the contemporary reader as does his fascination with the fantastic and with folk figures of the supernatural. Some readers confuse the very existence of such figures in Singer's work with a concern for traditional notions of religious transcendence and of sin and retribution. For them, Singer's use of supernatural images tends to obfuscate his thoroughly modern vision.

Hasidism and the Kabbalah, the same sources which provide Singer with the material which he transforms into a secular vision, are also the sources for the folk images of demons and angels which are found throughout his fiction. The Kabbalists developed an elaborate system of demonology, incorporating figures from medieval Arabic and Christian demonology as well as from Germanic and Slavic folklore. The demonology is full of human-made sources of evil, some produced when Adam slept with Lilith, chief of the female demons, others created each time sacred law is neglected. We are cautioned that if demons were always visible, their great numbers would astonish and horrify us. It seems that there are thousands to the right of us and thousands to the left.[4]

Humankind, abandoned by a distant God, is the impotent victim of consummate jokesters who, like the wanton boys and gods of *Lear*, tempt us to destruction. As the imp of "The Mirror" explains it: "When a demon wearies of chasing after yesterdays or of going round in circles on a windmill, he can install himself inside a mirror. There he waits like a spider in its web, and the fly is certain to be caught" (*Gimpel* 78). We are left to lament as did the Psalmist:

Why stand so far off, Lord,
    hiding thyself in time of need?
. . . .
    [The wicked man] lies in ambush in the villages
    and murders innocent men by stealth.
He is watching intently for some poor wretch;
he seizes him and drags him away in his net;
he crouches stealthily, like a lion in its lair
    crouching to seize its victim;
    the good man is struck down and sinks to the ground,
    and poor wretches fall into his toils.
He says to himself, "God has forgotten;
he has hidden his face and has seen nothing." (Ps. 10, 1–11)

    The link which the Psalmist makes between the presence
of evil and the absence of God is integral to the symbolism of
the Lurianic Kabbalah, in which evil is perceived to be a by-
product of God's removal of himself during the act of creation.
The Lurianic idea of *tzimtzum*, the contraction of *Ein-Sof*, or
the dimming of divine light, in the first stage of creation re-
sulted in a void or a place of darkness—both metaphors for
the realm of non-God or evil.[5] *Tzimtzum*, which is essentially
an act of divine exile, provides Singer with metaphoric connections between evil and the inaccessibility of God which
can be incorporated into a modern vision of his work. "The
material world," Singer has said, "is a combination of seeing
and blindness. This blindness we call Satan" (Farrell Lee,
"Seeing and Blindness" 157). While God and divine light are
Singer's metaphors for clarity of meaning—for "seeing"—
Satan, the dimming of divine light, and darkness indicate the
inaccessibility of meaning—or "blindness."[6] That God is absent, i.e., that meaning is denied us, is the evil, the darkness,
of the human condition.
    The Kabbalah relates that during the second stage of the
Lurianic creation myth, when the divine light or *sefirot* ema-
nated into the space provided for creation, the rays of light
grew ever more distant from *Ein-Sof*, and the world became
less and less spiritual and more and more material. The dregs

of the process, called the husks or shells (*kelippot*) are imagined as forces of evil. Here again, evil is imagined as the condition of being exiled at the farthest point from an ultimate source of meaning. Evil is the darkness or blindness of the human condition.

Thus, while Singer fills his fiction with a wide variety of folk figures—comic angels and imps, maliciously demonic narrators, dream phantoms and apparitions—the significance of the demonic in his fiction is always related, not to traditional notions of sin and retribution, but to his major theme of exile and the problem of meaning.

While some readers may be sidetracked by the issue of whether Singer personally believes in the occult and whether his use of it indicates concern for traditional religious ideas, others, in approaching Singer as a modern writer, may reduce his devils to no more than metaphors of psychological processes. The modern day demon is a function of the id, which, if not properly sublimated by the superego, can destroy the order upon which the ego, that cohesive sense of self, depends for all of its stability. In "Lost," Singer mischievously responds to those of his readers who refuse to accept his demons at face value: "Hidden powers that no one can explain exist everywhere. . . . But how long do [the newspapers] write about anything? Here in America, if the Heavens would part and the angel Gabriel were to fly down with his six fiery wings and take a walk on Broadway, they would not write about it for more than a day or two" (*Crown* 182). He asserts that "no other Yiddish writer writes about devils—or when they do, then only skeptically. . . . If I write about a devil, I treat him as though he exists; that's why I'm more a mystical than a symbolic writer" (Glanville 28).[7]

It is this insistence, in some stories, upon the substantive reality of supernatural forces which gives even his contemporary, urban settings their aura of a folk tradition. Singer's demons are forces of the irrational in that they operate beyond the limits of reason. But this is not to say that they function solely as manifestations of the psyche. Although they often are used as reflections of mental confusion, in some stories they also retain their autonomy as supernatural beings. For such stories to be fully understood, we must, while reading them, become like Gimpel, suspending our disbelief and accepting the fantastical as actual.

For example, "Alone"—which is typical of Singer's realistic fiction in characterization, setting, and theme—cannot be fully understood if the action is perceived as functioning simply in the mind of the narrator. Only because the demons of his mind have counterparts in the cosmos does his final renunciation of a she-devil acquire significance.

Amid the noise and confusion of a Miami Beach hotel, the narrator of "Alone" decides, as he has done many times before, that he would like to be alone. An imp must have overheard his wish because his hotel suddenly closes down and he is forced to find another, one which turns out to be his alone. So he receives his wish, but "in such a topsy-turvy way that it appeared the Hidden Powers were trying to show me I didn't understand my own needs" (*Friday* 48). Indeed, the misconception of his needs is the theme of the story. The solitude of the narrator proves to be burdensome: "Here before me, drenched in sunlight, was a summer melancholy. . . . Mankind, it seemed, had perished in some catastrophe, and I was left, like Noah—but in an empty ark, without sons, without a wife, without any animals" (50). He wearies of his fulfilled wish in very little time, for "who can play games in an empty world?" (51). And he decides that he was mistaken in his desires; what he needed all along was not total solitude but a woman:

> Like all forms of life, I, too, wanted to be fruitful, wanted to multiply—or at least to go through the motions. I was prepared to forget any moral or aesthetic demands. I was ready to cover my guilt with a sheet and to give way wholly, like a blind man, to the sense of touch. At the same time the eternal questions tapped in my brain: Who is behind the world of appearance? Is it Substance

with its Infinite Attributes? Is it the Monad of all Monads? Is it the Absolute, Blind Will, the Unconscious? Some kind of superior being has to be hidden in back of all these illusions. (51)

By expressing his new desire in terms of the command of the Deity to Adam to increase and multiply, the narrator humorously creates the counterpoint between physical desire and spiritual longing which is at the heart of many of Singer's stories.[8] The juxtaposition of the narrator's musings upon lovemaking with the series of "eternal questions" reveals his confusion as to the nature of his needs. Like other characters, he ponders the illusions of the world but does not question the misapprehensions which are so obviously his own. However, by declaring that he will forsake all moral and aesthetic laws, images of order which hold back the tides of chaos, the narrator invites the imps, ever ready for such an opportunity, to put him to the test, and in the process, they unwittingly force him to clarify his relationship with his God.

Singer's demonology is used to create a series of illusions which question the substance of every aspect of the external world while reflecting the befuddled interior of the narrator's mind. Confidence in the "reality" of the Miami Beach world is undermined as the large, bustling hotel in which the narrator has been living suddenly closes down, and he, reminiscing on his long since passed bachelor days, easily finds another smaller but empty one. Not only does this new world, so conveniently created just for him, seem to be a projection of his own mind, but the narrator's existence within the old world is suspect: "I was on Collins Avenue in Miami Beach, but I felt like a ghost, cut off from everything. I went into the library and asked a question—and the librarian grew frightened. I was like a man who had died, whose space had already been filled" (52). The world to which the narrator has been transported is one in which boundaries are amorphous: "There was no division, I felt, between the organic and the inorganic. Everything around me, each grain of sand, each pebble, was breathing, growing, lusting" (51).

However, a dichotomy is maintained, at least temporarily, between this new world and the "outside world":

> On the sea, oily-yellow near the shore, glossy-green farther out, a sail walked over the water like a shrouded corpse. Bent forward, it looked as if it were trying to call something up from the depths. Overhead flew a small airplane trailing a sign: MAR-GOLIES' RESTAURANT—KOSHER, 7 COURSES, $1.75. So the Creation had not yet returned to primeval chaos. They still served soup with kasha and kneidlach, knishes and stuffed derma at Margolies' restaurant. In that case perhaps tomorrow I would receive a letter. I had been promised my mail would be forwarded. It was my only link, in Miami, with the outside world. (52)

Perhaps the outside world has not yet returned to primeval chaos, but the demonic forces conjured up by the narrator's lack of faith and by his inability to understand his own motivations infiltrate his solitary, illusory domain. They come in storm:

> The palm trees looked petrified, expecting the onslaught. I hurried back toward my empty hotel, wanting to get there before the rain; besides, I hoped some mail had come for me. But I had covered barely half the distance when the storm broke. One gush and I was drenched as if by a huge wave. A fiery rod lit up the sky and, the same moment, I heard the thunder crack—a sign the lightning was near me. I wanted to run inside somewhere, but chairs blown from nearby porches somersaulted in front of me, blocking my way. Signs were falling down. The top of a palm tree, torn off by the wind, careened past my feet. I saw a second palm tree sheathed in sackcloth, bent to the wind, ready to kneel. (54–55)

The chaos created by the storm permeates the narrator's mind. He moves through the hurricane as through a dream or an Alice-in-Wonderland delusion:

> In my confusion I kept on running. Sinking into puddles so deep I almost drowned, I rushed forward with the lightness of boy-hood. The danger had made me daring, and I screamed and sang, shouting to the storm in its own key. By this time all traffic had

stopped, even the automobiles had been abandoned. But I ran on, determined to escape such madness or else go under. I had to get that special delivery letter, which no one had written and I never received. (55)

Throughout the story confidence in the outside world has been continuously undermined. Here the existence of his only concrete connection with an independent reality, the letter, "my only link . . . with the outside world," is threatened. And the substance of the narrator himself begins to disintegrate. He becomes as one with the storm, screaming in its own key, drowning in its puddles. When he finds his hotel, in a mirror his "half-dissolved image reflected itself like a figure in a cubist painting" (55). He is himself a figment of his own doubt, transmuted by the powers of the storm, whether within or outside of himself. He is ready for the test, set by forces of evil and by his own confused questioning. Thus, into his room enters the woman for whom he had wished and for whom he had said he would forsake any moral or aesthetic demands. She is the Cuban hunchback who manages his empty hotel:

I rested my head on the pillow and lay still with the eerie feeling that the mocking imp was fulfilling my last wish. I had wanted a hotel to myself—and I had it. I had dreamed of a woman coming, like Ruth to Boaz, to my room—a woman had come. Each time the lightning flashed, my eyes met hers. She stared at me intently, as silent as a witch casting a spell. . . . I wanted to pronounce an incantation against the evil eye and pray to the spirits who have the final word not to let this hag overpower me. Something in me cried out: *Shaddai*, destroy Satan. Meanwhile, the thunder crashed, the seas roared and broke with watery laughter. The walls of my room turned scarlet. In the hellish glare the Cuban witch crouched low like an animal ready to seize its prey—mouth open, showing rotted teeth; matted hair, black on her arms and legs; and feet covered with carbuncles and bunions. Her nightgown had slipped down, and her wrinkled breasts sagged weightlessly. Only the snout and tail were missing. (57–58)

The narrator is tempted by the Cuban demon as Zirel, who also lacked knowledge of herself, is tempted by the imp of "The Mirror." Zirel, blinded by boredom and vanity, is overcome by the forces of evil, but the narrator acknowledges God and is saved. When the Cuban hunchback says, "Who cares what you do? No one see [sic]" (59), she is not only tempting him sexually, she is confronting him with the eternal questions, which he had not been able to answer. His reply, "God sees," is a statement of faith which devitalizes the power of the demonic forces over him. He sleeps and when he awakens the storm has ceased, his hotel is closed, and "the Cuban woman looked at me crookedly—a witch who had failed in her witchcraft, a silent partner of the demons surrounding me and of their cunning tricks" (60).

The demons in "Alone" are forces of the irrational. However, although they function thematically as reflections of mental confusion, they nevertheless retain their autonomy as agents of other worlds. Obviously, Singer attempts to locate the demons of "Alone" in the narrator's psyche. The story is told by the protagonist. Through his eyes, both the familiar world of Miami Beach and his image of himself disintegrate, the storm menaces him, and the Cuban hunchback, "pale, thin, with her hair drawn back, and a glint in her black eyes . . . [wearing] an old-fashioned blouse edged with yellowed lace" (60), becomes an infernal witch. Her temptation of him occurs between a dream and a period of sleep. And the letter, which seems to be the only object of substance in an otherwise dissolving world, never materializes. The reply to his question at the conclusion of the story, "Isn't there a letter for me?," is "No letter" (60).[9]

But to make of the narrator's temptation only a psychological situation in which the demonic elements of the id surface momentarily is to diminish somewhat the impact of the story. Only because the demons of his mind have counterparts in the world outside of him does his final renunciation of the Cuban demon acquire significance. The narrator had stated

that he would forget any aesthetic or moral demands if only
he were granted a "hot-eyed woman," and the accommodat-
ing imps provide him with the Cuban "with black piercing
eyes." If her ugliness causes him to reject her, then his affirmation of transcendent meaning is merely a ruse, and the
temptation lacks significance. On the other hand, if his con-
science, that socioreligious structure of his superego, causes
him to reject her and to sublimate his desires, because not to
do so would be adulterous, then again the story fails, for
never does Singer imply that the narrator's dilemma lies in the
moral sphere. It is true that the narrator discovers that he
cannot renounce his aesthetic and moral scruples; he finds the
Cuban ugly and he remembers that he has a wife. But these
demands serve as additional indications of his self-deception
and as metaphors of structures which must be maintained
against disorder. When he declares that he is capable of re-
nouncing them, the forces of evil external to him infiltrate his
world and put him to the test. His temptation, therefore, is
more than a mental construct. The Cuban is indeed a demon,
not only a woman and not merely an hallucination. The psychological and the illusory are metaphors of his cosmic dilemma rather than the other way around. And the narrator's
disorientation amid the myriad illusions created by the imps
is a metaphor not only of a befuddled psyche but of a col-
lapsed cosmos.

In "A Wedding in Brownsville," not demons but a literal
portrayal of a kind of life after death must be accepted by the
reader if the story is to succeed as an aesthetic whole. In this
story, Dr. Solomon Margolin, agnostic survivor of the Holocaust, has been invited to a wedding by another survivor. He
travels by taxi, witnesses a fatal accident, and arrives at the
wedding to be reunited with a dead lover lost to him long ago
in the Nazi Holocaust.

The wedding frames the story from its opening line—"The
wedding had been a burden to Dr. Solomon Margolin from
the very beginning" (*Friday* 190)—to its closing—"With mea-
sured steps, Abraham Mekheles led his daughter down the

aisle" (206). Within this framework are three sequences which
evoke not the joy of a renewed commitment to life, which a
wedding represents, but rather a slow awakening to the inevitability of death. Hints of obliteration run throughout the
story, and each section interweaves images of both life and
death.

The first sequence plays upon the opening line, "The wedding had been a burden," to reveal the death of a marriage.
The day dawns "gray and dreary as dusk" (192) when Dr.
Margolin awakens and looks into the bathroom mirror, the
first of a series of introspective actions which bring him face to
face with death. A man who likes to "impress people with his
appearance" (195) and to disguise signs of age, he faces his
gray hair, deeply folded face, and exhausted baggy eyes.
Later, napping on his sofa, he reflects that "all his life . . . [he]
had been plagued by the eternal questions. . . . the fear of
death haunted even his dreams. Hitler's carnage and the ex-
tinction of his family had rooted out his last hope for better
days, had destroyed all his faith in humanity" (193–94).

Death clings to Dr. Margolin, to the sexual frigidity of his
marriage, and to his Gentile wife, Gretl, who "had her plot
waiting for her beside his in that part of the cemetery that the
Sencimeners had reserved for themselves" (193) and who,
in what can only be perceived as a death wish, "was forever
polishing the windows of their apartment on the sixteenth
floor . . . without using a safety belt" (194).

Gretl refuses to attend the wedding, and the couple's last
flat, petty interchange is one of lost hope. After refusing an
offered vitamin, Dr. Margolin says:

"Leave me alone."
"Well, it's your health, not mine."
And slowly she walked out of the room, hesitating as if she ex-
pected him to remember something and call her back. (195)

Dr. Margolin never does call her back, but he takes "a last
look in the mirror" (195) before leaving the house.

The second sequence comprises a symbolic and, as it turns

out, quite literal journey to death. Once in his taxi heading for
the wedding, Dr. Margolin peers out the window and, as if
already dead, cannot see outside, "There was nothing to
be seen" (196). The streets "sprawled out . . . impenetrably
dark":

> His destination was a wedding. Wasn't the world, like this taxi,
> plunging away somewhere into the unknown toward a cosmic
> destination? Maybe a cosmic Brownsville, a cosmic wedding?
> Yes. But why did God—or whatever anyone wanted to call him—
> create a Hitler, a Stalin? Why did He need world wars? Why
> heart attacks, cancers? Dr. Margolin took out a cigarette and lit it
> hesitantly. What had they been thinking of, those pious uncles of
> his, when they were digging their own graves? Was immortality
> possible? Was there such a thing as the soul? All arguments for
> and against weren't worth a pinch of dust. (196)

Amid the darkness, the thoughts of disease, death, and dust,
the taxi comes to a screeching, jolting collision, and a man is
carried off dead on a stretcher. The journey continues, but
with a difference, passing through a kind of Gehenna, the
"stubbornly silent" driver never uttering a word, driving
through unfamiliar streets filled with people "staring ahead
. . . eyes full of a gloomy hopelessness" and others in taverns
with "something unearthly about them, as if they were being
punished here for sins committed in another incarnation"
(197). Beyond a funeral parlor lies the wedding hall.[10]

The juxtapositions of life and death are intensified in the
second half of this sequence when, once at the wedding feast,
images of life and death alternate at a frenzied pace. The hall,
filled with music, dancing, flashing bulbs, pushing crowds,
"resounded with stamping, screaming, laughing, clapping"
(198), but just as fast-paced and insistent as these signs of life
are the constant reminders of death:

> "My father? He was killed. They were all killed. . . ." "Berish the
> son of Feivish? Starved to death in Russia. . . ." "Sorele? Shot. . . ."
> "Abraham Zilberstein? . . . A mound of charcoal was all that was
> left, coal and ash." "Yosele Budnik? He passed away years
> ago. . . ." "Your brother Chayim? Your Uncle Oyzer? They killed

everyone, everyone. . . ." "Riva herself? Where all the others
ended up: Auschwitz. How close we came ourselves! All of us are
really dead, if you want to call it that. We were exterminated,
wiped out. Even the survivors carry death in their hearts."
(198–99)

In the third sequence, during a joyful reunion with his first
love Raizel, who had been shot during the Holocaust, an
"eerie suspicion" (205) finally comes over Dr. Margolin. Slowly
he awakens to the fact of his own death—he was the victim of
the accident, his the dead body taken away, he the guest who
"still had not come" (199).

Images of life and death converge as the dead lovers look at
the wedding canopy and envision their own marriage. The
wedding which has framed this story of death is displaced
by death which frames another wedding—a wedding of the
dead. Like a double exposure in which two separate images
occupy one space, the dead and the living face the wedding
canopy—Dr. Margolin and Raizel hesitating on the threshold
of the chapel, Abraham Mekheles leading his daughter down
the aisle.

Typically, Singer shows space to be illusory, suggesting that
the dead exist not on a removed plane, but here in our own
space. The point is not to take this as a matter to believe or
disbelieve but to see instead that life and death are not ob-
verses; they do exist on the same plane, for there is indeed
much death in life, not merely in the graying hair and fur-
rowed brow of Dr. Margolin but in memories, in lost hope, in
sterile marriages. As the wedding guest says, "All of us are
really dead" (199).

But life can also arise from death. Thus, the renewed and
energizing love and hope of the dead Dr. Margolin and Raizel
who face the filled, yet hushed, wedding chapel becomes the
correlative of the Mekheles' wedding, which takes place in
spite of the death which almost overwhelms it and which defies the attitude of a guest who had asked, "Have you a son or
daughter to marry off? No? Well, it's better that way. What's
the sense of having children if people are such murderers?"

(199). Against a backdrop of death—of a marriage, of a man, of a litany of victims—a cantor intones benedictions, and Abraham Mekheles, survivor of the Holocaust, bravely leads his daughter down the aisle.

If one were to attempt to treat "A Wedding in Brownsville" psychologically and assume that Raizel is a hallucination which the quite live Dr. Margolin experiences while bombarded with memories of the dead, then the tightly rendered structure of this story and its sharp thematic contrasts would collapse. The accident scene and subsequent journey through death would be gratuitous, and the controlling design of the wedding framing death would lose its mirrored obverse of death framing the wedding. We must accept at face value the psychic phenomena in the story if its fullness is to be revealed.

In a story like "The Black Wedding," a perfect balance is maintained between demonic possession and psychological illness.[11] Here generations of the family of the Rabbi of Tzivkev are tormented by evil spirits in retaliation for the rabbi's exorcism of a dybbuk from a young girl. "The grandson, Rabbi Aaron Naphtali, had to contend with the vengeful devils all his life. He lit a candle, they extinguished it. He placed a volume on the bookshelf, they knocked it off. When he undressed in the ritual bath, they hid his silk coat and his fringed garment. . . . Once the rabbi laid his pen on the table and it sailed out through the open window as if carried by an unseen hand" (*Spinoza* 26–27). At his death, the rabbi cautions his daughter Hindele to keep silent, "if you are to be spared" (28).

The orphaned Hindele, sickly, with an "insane look in her black eyes" (28) is married off by the community to a divorced man with five chidlren.

When Reb Simon lifted the veil from Hindele's face after the wedding, she saw him for the first time. . . . He gazed at her like an animal. He breathed noisily and smelled of perspiration. Clusters of hair grew out of his nostrils and ears. His hands, too, had a growth of hair as thick as fur. The moment Hindele saw him she knew what she had suspected long before—that her bridegroom was a demon. . . . She wanted to call out "Hear, O Israel" but she remembered her father's deathbed admonition to keep silent. (30)

Hindele perceives the world around her as suffused with evil. The Chassidim are demons; their sashes, snakes; their sable hats, hedgehogs; their beards, clusters of worms; their Yiddish songs, the hissing of vipers. Ensnared within a "net of evil" Hindele becomes pregnant with a demon (32). Yet, true to her father's final words, never does she utter a sound, until at last, while giving birth, "a piercing scream tore itself from Hindele's throat and she was swallowed in darkness": "In Tzivkev and in the neighborhood the tidings spread that Hindele had given birth to a male child by Reb Simon of Yampol. The mother had died in childbirth" (35).

Whether the demons which Hindele sees are in the world about her or deep within herself does not matter in this story. The psychological horror of her situation, vividly rendered by the self-imposed exile of her silence, is the same in either case. If the demons are meant to exist literally, quite apart from her own perceptions of them, then Hindele has been hideously victimized and has had no way to cry out for help. And if she is mad, she nevertheless is shrouded in demonic horror, estranged from all around her, enmeshed in silence.

In "Taibele and Her Demon," the author does not want the reader to perceive the demon in the title as an actual devil. On the contrary, in this story it is necessary for us to realize that the demon is not real in order to understand why Taibele needs so much to believe that he is.

"One moonless summer evening when the town was as dark as Egypt," Taibele, a grass widow abandoned by her ascetic husband, tells her friends a tale about "a young Jewish woman, and a demon who had ravished her and lived with her as man and wife. Taibele recounted the story in all its details. The women huddled closer together, joined hands, spat to ward off evil, and laughed the kind of laughter that comes from fear" (*Friday* 3).

Alchonon, the teacher's helper, a bit of a devil himself, overhears the story and conceives of a mischievous prank. He visits Taibele that very night:

> She was almost asleep, when suddenly she saw a figure looming in the dark. She was too terrified to utter a sound.
> "Who is it?" she whispered, trembling.
> Alchonon replied in a hollow voice: "Don't scream, Taibele. If you cry out, I will destroy you. I am the demon Hurmizah, ruler over darkness, rain, hail, thunder, and wild beasts. I am the evil spirit who espoused the young woman you spoke about tonight. And because you told the story with such relish, I heard your words from the abyss and was filled with lust for your body. . . ." After a while, the demon got into Taibele's bed and had his will of her. (4–5)

Alchonon is at his best as a demon. By posing as Hurmizah two nights a week, he frees his imagination from all restraints, becoming a fanciful lovemaker and an inventive storyteller:

> Sometimes he pulled such pranks and babbled such devil's nonsense, that she was forced to laugh. He tugged at the lobe of her ear and gave her love-bites on the shoulder, and in the morning she found the marks of his teeth on her skin. He persuaded her to let her hair grow under her cap and he wove it into braids. He taught her charms and spells, told her about his night-brethren, the demons with whom he flew over ruins and fields of toadstools, over the salt marshes of Sodom, and the frozen wastes of the Sea of Ice. (7)

A fine line is drawn between how much Taibele knows about the nature of her demon and how much she needs to deceive herself:

> As the saying goes, may God preserve us from all that we can get accustomed to. And so it was with Taibele. In the beginning she had feared that her nocturnal visitant might do her harm. . . . Quite the contrary . . . Hurmizah entertained Taibele all through the night, and soon it came about that she began to miss him when he was away. The summer nights seemed too short, for Hurmizah would leave soon after cockcrow. Even

winter nights were not long enough. The truth was that she now loved Hurmizah, and though she knew a woman must not lust after a demon, she longed for him day and night. (6–8)

To recognize Hurmizah as human would be to admit that she was not forced to love him, that she had transgressed the law, that her "demon" is her own lust. Taibele "neither probed nor wished to probe too closely. She had long discovered that a devil had all the habits and frailties of a man. Hurmizah perspired, sneezed, hiccuped, yawned. Sometimes his breath smelled of onion, sometimes of garlic" (11).

One wintry night when Hurmizah comes to her sick, with sour breath and runny nose, with chills and fever, she listens as he leaves, "He had sworn to her that he flew out of the window even when it was closed and sealed, but she heard the door creak," and she prays, "There are so many devils, let there be one more" (12). But Hurmizah never visits her again. When she sees four pallbearers carrying the corpse of Alchonon, the teacher's helper, "a strange idea came to Taibele—to escort Alchonon, the feckless man who had lived alone and died alone, on his journey" (13).

Whereas in "The Black Wedding," Hindele was estranged from the world about her, here Taibele, "alone, doubly deserted—by an ascetic and by a devil" (14), is self-alienated because of her inability to admit even to herself that Alchonon was Hurmizah. "There are secrets that the heart cannot reveal to the lips" (14). Human beings, it seems, can be as great a riddle to themselves as the universe is to us all. Taibele's heart has a secret which is inaccessible to her own lips. Like the God who is silent, she, made in that image and likeness, has a silent, hidden part—a contraction of the heart.

In "Stories from Behind the Stove," a trio of storytellers try to top one another with tall tales. In these sly narratives, while characters wonder whether demons are responsible for the incredible happenings, the mystery of simple existence eludes them, and the mere talk of demons serves to divert even the reader from what is central to the text. One of the stories concerns a shed which mysteriously disappears, leaving no trace, only to reappear unexpectedly:

"Near Blonia there lived a man, Reb Zelig the bailiff. He had a store and a shed where he kept kindling wood, flax, potatoes, old ropes. He had a sleigh there too. He got up one morning and the shed was gone. He could not believe his eyes. If during the night there had been a wind, a storm, a flood! But it happened after Pentecost—calm days, quiet nights. At first he thought he had lost his mind. He called his wife, his children. They ran out. 'Where is the shed?' There was no shed. Where it had been, everything was smooth—high grass, no beams, shingles, no sign of a foundation. Nothing. Well, if the night creatures seize a man, they may have some claim, but what would they want with a shed? And how can grass grow up overnight? When they heard about this in Blonia, they ran as though to a fire. . . . They stood and stared at each other like graven images. People pinched their cheeks to make sure they were not dreaming. . . .

"Well, two weeks passed. Then early one morning Zelig came out of his house and saw the shed. He went wild—screamed and knocked his head. The whole household came out, barefoot, half naked. There stood the shed as if nothing had happened." *Kafka* (62–65)

The enlightened of the village—Falik the druggist, his wife, and Dr. Chalczynski—rejecting the popular opinion that demons were involved in the miracle of the shed, attempted in vain to discover a rational explanation for the phenomenon. While "the simple people had other things to worry about," the skeptics brooded, "If a shed can dissolve like snow, perhaps there is a God" (64).

A reason for the shed disappearing and reappearing is never established, but we are told that

"Falik and his wife were divorced. She married an elder from Sochaczew. Falik moved to Warsaw and converted to Christianity. One night Dr. Chalczynski left town. He didn't say goodbye to anybody—left behind all his books and instruments.

"I forgot the main thing. The shed burned down." (66)

For Zalman the glazier, who tells this story, the "main thing" is the miraculousness of the disappearing shed. Yet hidden within his story are all sorts of human mysteries of which the world is so full. Their very multiplicity renders them commonplace. Why did Falik and his wife divorce? Why did Falik become a Christian? Did the shed play a part in his conversion? Who was Dr. Chalczynski, this Gentile companion of enlightened Jews? Why is his disappearance less compelling than that of a shed?

Zalman and his listeners never wonder about these mysteries. Fixated on the fantastical, they fail to notice that human action and motivation can be as inexplicable as the disappearance of a shed.

In a related story, "Lost," Sam Opel tells the journalist narrator about his wife who was "born to lose and to be lost. She lost her money, her possessions, her fiancé. She might have lost [her] child, too, if she had not got lost herself" (*Crown* 191). Things would disappear before this woman's eyes—addresses, books, rings, her child's toys—until one day she, too, vanished utterly, leaving her husband to ask, "What does it mean? How can a thing become nothing? . . . I hoped that I would live long enough for the riddle to be solved, but I am at the end of my road and I have found no answer. A person who has witnessed what I did can no longer make plans, build a house, attach himself to people. Spiritually, I became lost myself" (191–92).

Here again, the fantastic, in the guise of the woman's fate, is treated as the central problem in the story and is finally attributed to demons. Yet the tale of the lost woman is secondary to the disregarded story hidden within the text. What, indeed, does it mean for a thing to disappear, to become nothing? What does it mean to be lost? Is the woman's disappearance not a form of death? In *Shosha*, Haiml Chentshimer asks concerning death: "How is it possible, after all, that someone should simply vanish? How can someone who lived, loved, hoped, and wrangled with God and with himself just disappear?" (269). To come to the end of one's life without a solution to the riddle of death is the predicament of every human being. Sam Opel is lost just as we are all lost, exiled in a world without answers, without explanations, equipped only with the question which Sam so plaintively asks, "What does it mean?"

It is in the darkness, at "the last station," exiled from a God who may not exist, that Ozer Mecheles of "On a Wagon" comes face to face with that very question as he enters the nether world of a spiritual and personal crisis:

> The summer night was warm and moonless. The conductor had put out the candles in the cars of the train as soon as the passengers stepped down, and the only light came from a kerosene lamp in the empty station. For a while, the locomotive puffed thick smoke, hissed, and poured water; then it began to move backward. Ozer caught a glimpse of the engineer. He stood at the window, half illuminated by the fire in the box, his face smeared with soot, like a chimney sweep. He made Ozer think of the black angels of Gehenna described in the Nod of Punishment. (*Crown* 295)

Unlike the substantive demons of "Alone" and other stories, here we have multiple suggestions of the demonic, setting the tone for the soul-shaking temptation and journey to death which Ozer is about to undergo. A traditional image of hell's fire and demons conjured up by the engineer, illuminated by the firebox, is preceded by more subtle allusions to the Kabbalic imagery of evil and exile. The moonlessness of the night is reminiscent of the Kabbalic connection of the disappearance of the moon with the exile of God,[12] and like the God who withdraws, dimming his divine light, the conductor puts out each candle, leaving a dark and empty station. The hissing locomotive, a mechanical demon of the industrial age, withdraws, leaving Ozer in exile, poised at the edge of the civilized world.

Singer has often explained the existence of evil in the world as necessary if humankind is to have the free will to choose.[13] Thus, often his characters are placed in situations of temptation—temptations which appear to be sexual, but which are more likely spiritual; temptations which appear to force a moral choice, but which are really insistent upon self-definition. In this story, as in "Alone," a sexual temptation is used to force Ozer to see more deeply into himself. A Hasid enticed by the Enlightenment, a faithful husband tempted sexually, a believer for whom the universe is a riddle, Ozer is confronted with a series of conflicts, each leading him closer to a central test.

The Yeshiva-trained Ozer is tempted by the worldly books of the Enlightenment, that movement of Jewish modernism which sought to purge Judaism of superstitution and folk influence. But try as he may to consider himself as one of the enlightened, with trips to Warsaw's museums and the study of "algebra, physics, [and] philosophy" (297), Ozer remains an unworldly Hasid, blushing when spoken to by women, losing himself in city streets, floundering on the telephone. "He had lived almost twenty-five years, he had read many scientific books, but the world remained as much a riddle to him as when he had started cheder" (298).

Once on the wagon which is to take him from the last station "through the night" to Zamość, he is tempted in the "half darkness" by Bella Felhendler, a woman who functions as did the Cuban demon of "Alone," moving Ozer from a sexual temptation to a test of faith. Her comic arguments for sexual transgression are interspersed with attacks on his belief:

> "A woman doesn't wear the same dress forever. You don't eat noodles with boiled beef every evening. . . . Why should God care if young people enjoy themselves? And how do you know there *is* a God? The delegate from Warsaw said that everything was evolution. He said that the earth was hot and it cooled off, like the crust on a pot of buckwheat. Is that true?"
> "Who knows."
> "I love Feivel. But if you love butter cookies, can't you eat a few macaroons?" (302–3)

Ozer's "Who knows" is reminiscent of yet quite different from the "God sees" with which the narrator of "Alone" had replied to his Cuban demon. That protagonist was able to clarify quite unequivocally his faith in God. Ozer's position, however, is more ambiguous. He does not know fully who he is nor what the world is. He possesses no certainty. The universe is a riddle to him. The one fixed point in his life has been his wife, Nesha, and Bella, by implying that Nesha might love another, slyly undermines his faith in her and in so doing undermines his faith in everything. The night, we are told, grows darker. The conflict between Ozer's Hasidic soul and his enlightened leanings merges with the loss of faith in his wife:

> Ozer was taking stock of his life. Yes, if one denies God, the Torah, and believes man has descended from an ape, why shouldn't one act like an ape? And if Nesha was so infatuated with Mendele Shmeiser, what value could he, Ozer, have for her? . . .
>
> . . . He raised his eyes to the sky. He had read the theory of Kant and Laplace that the universe developed from a nebula. But how can a nebula bring out man, animals, trees, grain, flowers, eyes, ears, a brain? . . . Somewhere Ozer Mecheles had made a false calculation, but where was the error? Could he become pious again? . . . In what can he believe?
>
> Fate? Was it Mendele's fault his atoms combined in this way instead of another? And how is it Nesha's fault? How can there be talk of good and evil if there is no God, no revelation?
>
> Ozer Mecheles closed his eyes. He did not sleep but neither was he awake. A heaviness pressed on his heart, hanging there like a weight. He was cold, as though it were winter. He felt like a mourner: he had to sit shivah for his own illusions. (304–6)

Ozer Mecheles has lost everything on this journey which has awakened him to the fact of his own spiritual death. He mourns his beliefs and his struggles to believe. Arriving in Zamość, he goes to the study house. "Here the night still held sway. . . . Ozer stopped and tried to read the Ten Commandments in the dusk, but the letters were hidden" (307). Again Singer reminds us of the darkness of the night—metaphor of evil, of the exile of divine light. Darkness defines the human condition as devoid of revelation, without meaning. Such darkness prevents Ozer from reading the Ten Commandments, for in the darkness of God's absence, in the vacuity of meaning, "how can there be talk of good and evil?" Moreover, for Singer, language is the new source of transcendent meaning, and in the Kabbalah, each letter of the alphabet holds mystical power, but here in the dark night of the study house, these very letters are hidden.

Thus, while standing in the place where once he could find meaning through faith, Ozer finds himself alone in the darkness of a silent universe, exiled from every possibility of meaning. "A weariness such as he had never experienced overcame him" (307). Ozer has come to that point in life which Camus describes in the life of his everyman: "One day the 'why' arises and everything begins in that weariness tinged with amazement. 'Begins'—this is important. Weariness comes at the end of the acts of a mechanical life, but at the same time it inaugurates the impulse of consciousness" ("Absurd Reasoning" 10).

From out of this dark night of the soul which has obliterated all hope of transcendence and left him as one dead, like "the corpses [which] are supposed to pray in the holy places, before the first worshipper crosses the threshold" (307), dawn comes, bringing forth the light of revelation:

Suddenly a purple light blasted through the windows and everything in the study house was illuminated as though from a heavenly lamp: the lectern, the benches, the stands, the lions on the cornice of the Holy Arc that were supporting the tablets with their curled tongues. Their beady eyes seemed alive. Ozer stood transfixed. It became clear as the rising day to him that the books he had brought from Warsaw and the Commandments on these tablets denied one another. If creation was a blind process and man a beast, it was allowed to deceive Ozer (or Feivel), steal from him, even kill him. Why didn't I understand it before? he wondered. He shuddered and his teeth rattled. For the first time in years, he had a desire to start the morning with a prayer, but how could he be sure that his prayer would be heard?

Ozer went outdoors. In the sky, a cloud like a fiery chariot rode toward the east. The windows of the synagogue shone and flickered. The water in the barrel had become greenish, and

Ozer saw his image in it as in a mirror: a pale face, sunken cheeks, two sidelocks like hemp, a throat with a pointed Adam's apple. He barely recognized himself. The worldliness was gone. He was again what he had been before his marriage to Nesha—a poor scholar from Lublin, an orphan supported by strangers. He bent down and dipped his fingers in the water. Powers stronger than man had conspired to take everything from him this night: his wife, his dowry, his lodging. The Enlightenment had deceived him; Nesha and Mendele Shmeiser did the rest. Ozer knew he must again pack a bundle and make his way somewhere to a yeshiva. He was not angry, only astonished. He had to make a choice between God, Who may not exist, and creatures as loathsome as Mendele Shmeiser and his females. (307–8)

The religious imagery in this long passage supports not a religious apotheosis but a personal resurrection. Ozer Mecheles, who has journeyed into death, sat shivah for his own illusions, and come like a corpse to the studyhouse, finally is reborn into a new vision. Ozer finally sees, not God, but himself. He sees his own image as in a mirror and finds it barely recognizable. But he has come to understand the contradictions between Hasidism and the Enlightenment, between belief and disbelief, which he has harbored within himself. Although Ozer's world has been shattered, he finally comprehends the choice which he must make if he is to clarify the vision he has had of himself in the murky waters of the rain barrel. With a weariness tinged with astonishment, Ozer Mecheles must choose not between God and the world but between a God who may not exist and the world. He stands alone—open-eyed, honest, heroic—poised on the brink of two abysses. All that is clear is the necessity of choice.

Choice is crucial for Ozer Mecheles and for each of Singer's meditants. Exiled from any meaning that is sanctioned from on high, they are finally left possessed only of the free will necessary to create for themselves the meaning they seek. In discussion, Singer habitually associates free will with the second stage of the Kabbalah's creation myth, during which the emanating light of *Ein-Sof* grew ever more distant from its source and the darkness of evil became apparent:

In the higher worlds, says the Cabala, there is no free will because they are so near to God. The difference between them and God is not great enough that there should be temptations or desire for sin. Everything is done according to heavenly will. Only here in this prison, in this dark den, where Satan and all the devils rule, only here does man have free will. He can choose between life and death, between evil and good, between wisdom and foolishness, and so on and so on. (Farrell Lee, "Seeing and Blindness" 154)[14]

Although the questioning nature of humankind rails against the darkness which defines our human exile from meaning, it is that very darkness which is a necessary constituent of our humanity. Without darkness, it seems, there would be no need for the freedom through which we can define ourselves. Singer's devils are personifications of that darkness, appearing suddenly in our lives, tempting, forcing choices. The pattern of temptation in Singer's stories, then, is concerned not with traditional moral issues, but rather, the temptations and the demons serve to define existential and ontological issues, to force humankind, at the least, to experience the darkness of exile and, better yet, to attempt to define meaning and value in the midst of that darkness.

4   *Mythic Dimensions of Exile*

Community, Part One

In "The Last Demon," a devil narrator tells us how a rabbi has but one weapon with which to defend himself from the demonic: "'That means you're a devil. *Pik*, get out of here,' the rabbi cries. He races to his bookcase, pulls out the *Book of Creation* and waves it menacingly over me. What devil can withstand the *Book of Creation?* I run from the rabbi's study with my spirit in pieces" (*Friday* 129).

The *Book of Creation*, which so magically wards off evil spirits, is a variant translation of the title of the *Sefer Yezirah*, the *Book of Formation*, that Kabbalic text which speculates on the creation of the world through the emanating light and logos of *Ein-Sof*.[1]

The *Book of Creation* is such a virulent threat to the demon because, in the mythic worldview from which Singer draws his imagery, creation and the demonic are primal and deadly opposites. The demonic personifies the void which the fullness of creation threatens to negate, the chaos forever menaced by God's formal order, the darkness opposed by God's light, the silence obliterated by God's word. It is meaninglessness and death overshadowed by revelation and life; it is exile ended by redemption.

"*Save us*," chants a mother demon in "Shiddah and Kuziba," "*From Light, from Words.*" Her son screams out in terror when he sees light, but his mother, married to a devil who studies the secret of silence, assures him that "a time would come when the light of the Universe would be extinguished.

All the stars would be snuffed out; all voices, silenced; all surfaces, cut off." She prays, *"Lord of All Silence / Destroy the
Din" (Spinoza* 92, 95). Such is the yearning from the abyss.

The creation of life and light, the revelation of meaning,
should destroy the demons of darkness and silence and insig-
nificance. However, with the retreat of *Ein-Sof* in the primal
act of creation, humankind finds itself exiled from the ultimate source of light and logos and enmeshed instead in darkness and silence. Ever since the "breaking of the vessels" during the emanation of the *sefirot* into the space provided for
creation, and the subsequent scattering of "divine sparks," all
of creation has been in exile.

To redeem itself from this exile, to find meaning in the darkness, humankind, replaying countless myths, can ritualistically repeat and thereby reassert the primal action of creation
by forming out of the chaos a microcosm of divine order.
Community is the form which this microcosm takes.

Mircea Eliade, in his transcultural studies of the nature of
religion, makes clear the sacral importance of forming community. For traditional societies such acts were "only repeti-
tion of a primordial act, the transformation of chaos into cosmos by the divine act of creation. When they tilled the desert
soil, they were in fact repeating the act of the gods who
had organized chaos by giving it a structure, forms, and
norms" (31). As Yahweh, victorious over the forces of the
abyss, brought forth light out of the darkness, forming order
from chaos, so humankind, by adhering to the law of the
Torah and by performing religious ritual "raises up" the divine
sparks scattered throughout the world, restoring harmony to
the universe.

Community, then, is a force of profoundly mythic proportions.[2] It is intimately connected, through the imagery of the
Kabbalah, with the divine drama of creation, exile, and redemption. In Kabbalic texts, the Community of Israel is identified with the *Shekhinah*, the tenth of the emanating *sefirot*.[3]
This *sefira* is representative of the very immanence or face of
Ein-Sof. The exile of the *Shekhinah* from *Ein-Sof* during the

act of creation symbolizes the exile of Israel from its God, and
the reunion of *Ein-Sof* and the *Shekhinah* is analogous to the
redemption of Israel from its exile.

The Kabbalah describes the redemptive process (called *tik-
kun*) as a process of restoration, wherein, by prayerfully maintaining religious precepts, each scattered spark of divine light
is mystically "raised up," released from its exile and restored
to the original harmony intended by *Ein-Sof.*[4] By maintaining
the religious community through adherence to the law, humankind can reverse the process of cosmic exile, restore harmony to the universe and redeem not only itself but all of
creation.[5] As Scholem writes: "Israel's state is symbolic of the
state of creation as a whole. It is the Jew who holds in his
hands the key to the *tiqqun* of the world, consisting of the
progressive separation of good and evil by the performance of
the commandments of the Torah" (*Sabbatai Sevi* 42).

But, as Bagdial, the angel in charge of "The Warehouse,"
complains with some resentment, after scratching "the nape
of his neck with one of his lower wings and [brooding] in silence," restoring the divine creation to its intended harmony
by keeping communal order is an overwhelming burden:

"He created the world in six short winter days and has been rest-
ing ever since. There are those who are of the opinion that He
didn't even work that hard."

"Do you mean by that that He wasn't the First Cause?" the
philosopher demanded.

"Who else is the First Cause? He is a jealous God. He would
never delegate such power. But being the cause and keeping
order are different things altogether." (*Seance* 134)

"Keeping order" would seem to be an impossible task, for
the forces of darkness and chaos continually infiltrate Singer's
fictional worlds, destroying community by disrupting the traditions of order, the laws and ancient rituals which define the
relationships among people and between humankind and God.
Dietary laws are not observed, ritual baths are not attended,
prohibitions against the mingling of men and women are ig-

nored, and the rules surrounding marriage are disregarded.[6] The regulations of faith stay the forces of evil, preserve the order of the community, and ritualistically recreate the primal orderings of creation. Once unheeded, chaos ensues. The mythic paradigm is endlessly repeated. The demonic battle against order is won only to be lost; the struggle is renewed, won, lost again.

This cycle is played out in "The Gentleman from Cracow," in which a false messiah ingratiates himself into the poor community of Frampol, spreading wealth and slowly undermining the rituals of faith. Finally, the gentleman proposes one day that every young woman of the village must marry before midnight without the seven-day waiting period and the prescribed ablutions. The townspeople acquiesce, and in a pandemonium of movement and music, the mismatched marriages take place: "Fiddles screeched, drums pounded, trumpets blared. The uproar was deafening. Twelve-year-old boys were mated with 'spinsters' of nineteen. The sons of substantial citizens took the daughters of paupers as brides; midgets were coupled with giants, beauties with cripples" (37). The chaos recreated out of the community becomes explicit after the handsome doctor from Cracow takes the witch Hodle, daughter of Lipa the Ragpicker, as bride:

> Now, as though the powers of darkness had been summoned, the rain and hail began to fall; flashes of lightning were accompanied by mighty thunderclaps. But, heedless of the storm, pious men and women embraced without shame, dancing and shouting as though possessed. Even the old were affected. In the furor, dresses were ripped, shoes shaken off, hats, wigs and skullcaps trampled in the mud. Sashes, slipping to the ground, twisted there like snakes. Suddenly there was a terrific crash. A huge bolt of lightning had simultaneously struck the synagogue, the study house, and the ritual bath. The whole town was on fire. (*Gimpel* 38)

Not only are the sacred prohibitions regarding marriage ignored, but the townspeople in frenzy and hysteria imitate the storm created by the powers of darkness. Even clothing seems possessed—sashes writhe like snakes. In the resulting apocalyptic fire, every edifice of the law is annihilated.

The threat posed by Frampol's lapse in faithful adherence to the law is rendered by Singer as an assault on the community by the forces of chaos.[7] The gentleman from Cracow reveals himself to be not

> the young man the villagers had welcomed, but a creature covered with scales, with an eye in his chest, and on his forehead a horn that rotated at great speed. His arms were covered with hair, thorns, and elflocks, and his tail was a mass of live serpents, for he was none other than Ketev Mriri, Chief of the Devils.
>
> Witches, werewolves, imps, demons, and hobgoblins plummeted from the sky. (39)

Singer's devils invade the world, and with a power which sometimes seems coextensive with that of the Creator of order, they recreate the cosmos in their own diabolical image and likeness. The gentleman from Cracow transforms the village of Frampol into a Boschian landscape of Hell:

> Never before had Frampol seen such a sunset. Like rivers of burning sulphur, fiery clouds streamed across the heavens, assuming the shapes of elephants, lions, snakes, and monsters. They seemed to be waging a battle in the sky, devouring one another, spitting, breathing fire. It almost seemed to be the River of Fire they watched, where demons tortured the evil-doers amidst glowing coals and heaps of ashes. The moon swelled, became vast, blood-red, spotted, scarred, and gave off little light. The evening grew very dark, dissolving even the stars. The young men fetched torches, and a barrel of burning pitch was prepared. Shadows danced back and forth as though attending a ball of their own. (34–35)

The sunset of Frampol embodies within itself the chaotic forces of evil, which infuse violent movement into the shapes and colors of the sky, recreating the primordial battle of the heavens. Hellish phantoms introduce both a darkness and a fire so intense that even the stars dissolve. The young men— who are involved in an unauthorized ball, a transgression against the law—seek, in a symbolic reenactment of the first creation, to rekindle light; but, enmeshed as they are in the forces of disorder, they succeed only in creating still more malefic beings in the shadows which play upon the walls, mimicking and mocking the dance.

The reenactment of the primal battle between God and Satan, cosmos and chaos, is vividly portrayed as the waters, once separated from the firmament in Genesis, are fused back into the land. The people of Frampol, tempted and subjugated by the demonic, are sucked into the resulting sludge:

> There was nothing but one great swamp, full of mud, slime, and ashes. Floundering in mud up to their waists, a crowd of naked people went through the movements of dance. At first, the rabbi mistook the weirdly moving figures for devils, and was about to recite the chapter, "Let there be contentment," and other passages dealing with exorcism, when he recognized the men of his town. Only then did he remember the doctor from Cracow, and the rabbi cried out bitterly, "Jews, for the sake of God, save your souls! You are in the hands of Satan! . . .
>
> But everything had turned to mud; the town of Frampol, stripped and ruined, had become a swamp. Its inhabitants were mud-splashed, denuded, monstrous. For a moment, forgetting their grief, they laughed at each other. The hair of the girls had turned into elflocks, and bats were entangled there. The young men had grown gray and wrinkled; the old were yellow as corpses. (40–42)

Frampol is destroyed, and in the holocaust, her children are slaughtered. But as humankind was created from the dust of the earth, so out of the slime of Frampol a new generation is born, a new town is built, and a new order is created.

The ease with which the gentleman from Cracow inspires a messianic delusion in the villagers of Frampol is the measure of their intense human need for transcendence. In Singer's first novel, *Satan in Goray*, that longing for transcendence and the inability to find it is interwoven with an imaginative portrayal of an historical event of messianism, the appearance in the seventeenth century of the false messiah, Sabbatai Sevi.

The Sabbatian movement surpassed any other messianic heresy in Jewish history, originating in Palestine and extending throughout the Mideast and Europe.[8] It officially began in May 1665 when Sabbatai Sevi declared himself the messiah and persisted even after he chose, in September 1666, while captive of the Turks, to convert to Islam rather than to die.

Sabbatai might have remained an obscure eccentric if his messianic delusions had not been affirmed by Nathan of Gaza, a brilliant and respected scholar of the Kabbalah, who had been born in Jerusalem but who lived with his wife in Gaza. In 1665, he experienced a prophetic awakening and declared Sabbatai Sevi to be the messiah. As a result of Nathan's proselytizing, the Sabbatian movement coalesced and spread.

In *Satan in Goray,* Singer maintains the general historical background of the movement, displacing specific historical facts into a variety of characters and details. However, the historical dimension of the novel is subordinant to its mythical context. Just as the gentleman from Cracow's intrusion into the community of Frampol was the vehicle for Singer's vision of the mythic struggle between the forces of creation and those of chaos, so too is the Sabbatian movement into Goray the means by which he explores the efficacy of community as a mystical source of meaning which can transcend the darkness personified by the demonic.

The first half of the novel establishes, amid rumors of Sabbatai Sevi's appearance, the significance of community. Goray is representative of a sacred, communal order, juxtaposed to the wild and threatening chaos which surrounds it.[9] Like a refrain defining its exile, Goray is repeatedly described as "the town that lay in the midst of the hills at the end of the world" (3).[10] "Goray had always been isolated from the world. Hills and dense woods extended for miles about the town. Winters, the paths were the lurking-place of bears, wolves, and boars. Since the great slaughter the number of wild beasts had multiplied" (5).

The "great slaughter" refers to the last demonic descent

upon the town—the atrocious massacres in 1648 by the Ukrainian Chmelnicki. Singer's initial paragraph describes with historical accuracy the Cossack's murderous attack upon the Jews:

> They slaughtered on every hand, flayed men alive, murdered small children, violated women and afterward ripped open their bellies and sewed cats inside. Many fled to Lublin, many underwent baptism or were sold into slavery. . . . the prayer house and the study house were filled with dung left by the horses that the soldiers had stabled there. . . . corpses lay neglected in every street, with no one to bury them. Savage dogs tugged at dismembered limbs, and vultures and crows fed on human flesh. (3–4)[11]

Goray, which "had been known for its scholars and men of accomplishment," now seemed "erased forever" by these forces of evil, which, not content to murder, desecrated both human life and the sacred edifices of Jewish community (4).

Following the mythic cycle of destruction and renewal, Goray, like Frampol, which was reconstructed from the ashes of its own damnation, begins to repopulate itself, for "it is the way of the world that in time everything reverts to what it has been" (4).

Rabbi Benish Ashkenazi returns to Goray to reconsecrate the community by reinstituting sacred law. "He moved immediately into his old house, near the prayer house, began to supervise the observance of the laws of ritual diet, saw to it that the women went to the ritual bathhouse at the proper time, and that young men studied the Torah" (5). But Rabbi Benish, who battles all who seek to destroy the religious community, whose very shadow engages in "ghostly wrangle[s]" (47) and who punishes a student who "isolate[s] himself from the community" (25), becomes himself a recluse, sitting alone, locked within his study, helpless in the face of bitter divisions within his family, unable to form community within his own household.

A chapter contrasting the old and the new Goray juxtaposes the images of disruption which permeate Benish's home with those which pervade the newly established community. The chapter begins with an image of a debased Goray immersed in darkness, sunk in mud, where "they lit no lamps at night" and where "women in mannish boots, their heads covered with torn shawls . . . crawl forth . . . like worms emerging from their holes" (28). The old Goray, introduced with the phrase "once upon a time" (29), seems as insubstantial as a fairy tale. Then, "everything had proceeded in an orderly fashion" (29), "community needs" (33) were fulfilled, but now, in the new Goray, "every man went his own way, no longer willing to share the common responsibility" (34).

Paralleling this social dissolution of the community, an "interminable family quarrel" (14) which pits brother against brother, mother against son, infects Benish's household. There the rabbi's son and daughter-in-law "like two great spiders spinning an evil web, sat apart from the rest in a pique in their darkened room, where the curtains were always drawn and the door always closed" (35). The images of worms and spiders which enclose this chapter are harbingers of Satan who, serpentine and veiled by cobwebs, later makes his apocalyptic entrance into Goray. Moreover, they serve to link the familial and social schisms in Goray with the later, more violent assaults upon the town. When "the Evil One triumphs" over Goray and the messianic hopes are finally dashed, these schisms become more apparent. "Wild bloody" battles between factions ensue. They find their metaphor in "a fault [which] was discovered in the prayer-house wall, extending from the roof to the foundation . . . it was rumored to be unsafe to worship there, since the walls might collapse" (191). Thus, the very core of communal order is destroyed.

Such assaults on the community are prefigured by the entry into Goray of a messenger from Yemen, "darting fiery glances" (40) and announcing, in the context of the final battle of the universe, the coming of the messiah: "The Jews from the other side of the river Sambation are ready and waiting for the battle of Armageddon. . . . The lion that dwelleth on high will descend from Heaven, in his mouth a seven-headed scorpion. . . . With fire issuing from his nostrils, he will carry the Messiah into Jerusalem. Gather your strength, O Judeans, and make yourselves ready!" (41–42). This cosmic battle is mirrored in the community by a war between the Orthodox Rabbi Benish and the Cabalist Mordecai Joseph, "a faster, a weeper, an angry man" (42), who hates Benish "for his learning, envied him his fame, and never missed an opportunity to speak evil of him" (48). Mordecai Joseph, a kind of debased Nathan of Gaza, has a vision of Sabbatai Sevi and declares him to be the messiah:

> The flame crackled and hissed, red shadows danced on the irregular whitewashed walls, and the rafters loomed low. In a corner, on a pile of rags, sat Mordecai Joseph's only daughter, a monstrosity with a water-swollen head and calf's eyes. Mordecai Joseph's wet beard shone in the reflection of the glowing coals like molten gold, and his green eyeballs burned like a wolf's as he divulged the mysteries he had seen in his trance. His cadence was that of a dying man speaking his last words to those nearest him. (39)

Although later, after Satan triumphs in Goray, Mordecai Joseph is transformed into a hero, here he is clearly associated with a monstrous vision, as hellish as the crackling, hissing fire and the specter of the apocalypse which he ultimately offers his followers. He epitomizes the demonic forces against which Rabbi Benish, as consecrator of the community, must fight. Their first skirmish takes place in the rabbi's absence. Benish's charity student is beaten senseless in a scapegoat ritual by Mordecai Joseph and his followers. In a scene of demonic proportions, with blood shed in the study house, Mordecai Joseph calls upon this evil as a witness to God: "Thus rotteth the name of the wicked! . . . Now he shall know that there is a God who rules the world!" (51)[12]

Benish's second and final battle is clearly waged against the demonic. He "prepares for war with the Sabbatai Zevi sect" (96), but "the others" (103) arrive to defeat him. "The others"

are the demonic forces of disorder which penetrate inwardly
to pervade every aspect of Goray's social and psychological
order and are reflected outwardly in storm—storm which becomes malicious, striking down Rabbi Benish as he attempts
to stop a ball, a profanation against the law:

> "A whole crowd of men and women have gathered together! At
> Reb Eleazar Babad's, on the upper floor! Men dancing with
> women. Profanations!" . . . Weak-kneed, Rabbi Benish pulled up
> his collar. He expected darkness outside, but it was bright as twi-
> light. An icy wind immediately gripped him and took his breath
> away. Thin needles of snow or rain—it was impossible to tell
> which—began to sting his face, which immediately swelled. . . .
> all at once a great hoarse wind rushed upon him, thrusting him
> back several steps, and began to drive him downhill from be-
> hind. . . . Casting a terrified glance over his shoulder, Rabbi Be-
> nish realized that evil was abroad and tried to return to his house.
> But at that moment his eyes were filled with sand. . . . Suddenly
> the storm seized him, bore him aloft for a short distance, as on
> wings, and then cast him down with such violence that in the tur-
> moil he could hear his bones shatter. (105–7)

Although, in the order of creation, "the Lord on high is
mightier far / than the noise of great waters, / mightier than
the breakers of the sea" (Ps. 93:4), here, in Singer's world,
storm, as the power of chaos, is resurgent throughout the
landscape. It is not the whirlwind out of which God speaks
nor a divine force of nature like the great flood of Noah which
punished and admonished humankind for transgressions
against the Almighty. Nor is it the objective correlative of a
Gothic landscape which mirrors the violent emotions of the
characters. Rather, it is a cosmic force of demonism infusing
nature with vicious, chthonic vitality, "barking at the Creator"
("Alone," *Friday* 55) and obstructing his rabbi from restoring
order in the community. "Storm . . . instead of separating the
waters as in the creative act, reduces all things to primitive
chaos, as if in a fury of uncreation" (Ricoeur 185).[13] While in
Genesis, God separated the land from the sea and calmed the

watery abyss, storm, in a riot of uncreation, "overflow[s] the shores and float[s] the land away" ("Alone," *Friday* 55).

Left feverish and delirious with pain, Rabbi Benish, for whom "everything seemed suddenly to be amiss" (112), abandons his community, like the God who retreats from his creation, leaving behind those who scream after him, "Holy Rabbi, why do you forsake us? Rabbi! Ho-ly Rabbi!" (118). The villagers' cry concludes the first half of the novel and stands at the thematic center of this and all of Singer's work. It is representative of the universal human cry of anguish in the face of exile; it expresses the abandonment humankind feels, lost in a world from which God has withdrawn.

As the godly retreat of *Ein-Sof* heralded the forces of darkness, so Rabbi Benish's retreat from Goray opens the community up to the fullest invasion of the demonic. Singer uses those Kabbalic images of exile and redemption which were closely associated with the Sabbatian movement to reveal the magnitude of this demonic invasion of the community. The Kabbalah relates that during the emanation of the *sefirot*, when the "breaking of the vessels" occurred, divine sparks of light adhered to the broken fragments of the vessels. The fragments are called the husks, shards, or shells (*kelippot*) and constitute the forces of evil.[14] Within each husk is imprisoned a spark of divine light which, in the process of redemption, must be released from its exile to return to its source in *Ein-Sof*.

Because of its association with the Community of Israel, the exile and redemption of the tenth *sefira*, the *Shekhinah*, becomes of greatest importance in the Kabbalah and in the messianism of Sabbatai Sevi. The *sefirot*, those attributes or names of *Ein-Sof*, are pictorialized and personified in the Kabbalah, and in a significant departure from previous rabbinical conceptions of the *Shekhinah*, this *sefira*, the immanence or face of God, is personified as feminine.[15] In fact, the symbolic language of the Kabbalah refers to the exile of the *Shekhinah* as the separation of a bride from her husband: "Only with the advent of messianic redemption will the perfect unity of the divine *sefiroth* be permanently re-established. Then . . . the Shekhinah will be restored to perpetual union with her husband" (Scholem, *Sabbatai Sevi* 17).[16]

Everywhere sparks of the *Shekhinah* are scattered, exiled in the shards of creation, awaiting deliverance. "The reunion of God and His *Shekhinah*," Scholem writes, "constitutes the meaning of redemption" (*On the Kabbalah* 108). In Sabbatai's reinterpretation of the Kabbalah, the messiah must descend into the realm of evil in order to release the *Shekhinah* from the *kelippot:*[17]

> Evil existed by virtue of the vitality which it drew from the sparks of good that it had snatched and held imprisoned. Once these sparks were released and "raised," evil, impotent and lifeless as it is by itself, would automatically collapse. At this point, Sabbatian doctrine introduces a dialectical twist into the Lurianic idea. According to the new, Sabbatian version, it is not enough to extract the sparks of holiness from the realm of impurity. In order to accomplish its mission, the power of holiness—as incarnate in the messiah—has to descend into impurity, and good has to assume the form of evil. (Scholem, *Sabbatai Sevi* 801)

As Itche Mates the Packman puts it, while "divulging mysteries of mysteries" to the townspeople of Goray: "Only a few holy sparks still burned among the husks of being. The powers of darkness clung to these, knowing that their existence depended on them. Sabbatai Zevi, God's ally, was battling these powers; it was he who was conducting the sacred sparks back to their primal source" (72).

It is probable that the Sabbatian movement did not collapse after Sabbatai's apostasy because what seemed to be his betrayal of Judaism was instead incorporated into his new version of the Kabbalah. But his mission was, as Scholem writes, "fraught with danger . . . only the complete transformation of good into evil would exhaust the full potential of the latter and thereby explode it, as it were, from within. This dialectical liquidation of evil requires not only the disguise of good in the form of evil but total identification with it" (*Sabbatai Sevi* 801).

In *Satan in Goray*, this drama of mythic proportions is played out on the battlefield of the mundane. Through multiple allusions, the *Shekhinah*—exiled *sefira*, face and immanence of *Ein-Sof*, Community of Israel—is seen to be incarnate in the person of Rechele, a daughter of Goray.[18]

Using historical parallels, Singer associates Rechele with Sabbatai Sevi's wife while simultaneously—yet far more subtly—he draws, almost as a veiled shadow of the historical parallels, a mythic portrait of her as the exiled *Shekhinah*. As a child, Rechele was blessed by her uncle who, laying his hands upon her head, said, "May the Lord make thee as Sarah, Rebecca, Rachel, Leah" (50). These four names allude to Rechele's historical and mythical analogues. Sarah and Rebecca are names associated with Sabbatai's wife, Rachel and Leah with the *Shekhinah*.

The historical person of Sarah, Sabbatai Sevi's third and most influential wife, is hidden beneath layers of conflicting legends concerning her mysterious origins, her great beauty, her promiscuous and sometimes bizarre behavior, her visions, and her witchcraft. She became the prophetess of the Sabbatian movement and often used as her signature the symbolic name bestowed upon her by Nathan of Gaza—"the Lady Queen Rebekah" (Scholem, *Sabbatai Sevi* 192).[19]

Clearly Rechele is drawn along the lines of Sarah. Beautiful and half-mad, given to visions and wild laughter, Rechele becomes the prophetess of Goray and the wife of Sabbatai's fictional counterparts. Sarah was orphaned during the Chmelnicki massacres; Rechele was born just weeks before them and was left upon her mother's death at the home of an uncle and his mother-in-law. Her childhood is one of sheer terror; all the nightmares ever dreamt by any child seem to come true in Rechele's young life. Real events merge with folktales and religious drama to create a surreal world as hellish as any Singer has imagined: the blood, gore, bulging eyeballs of beasts slaughtered in her uncle's yard, the waxy touch and widening grin of her "granny's" corpse, the feel of "dead" hands running over her body "with impure delight," mix with tales of "man-eaters that roasted children on spits," and a terrified, child-eyed vision of Yom Kippur eve (59). Rechele's childhood traumas leave her as "one apart. She was beset by mysterious ills. Some said she suffered from the falling sickness, others that she was in the power of demons" (68). References associating Rechele with the *Shekhinah* are sometimes playfully hidden in the text. For instance, here, with an impish allusion to the fall of the sparks of the *Shekhinah* into the creative void where, exiled, she remains trapped by the *kelippot*, we read of Rechele's "falling sickness" and her imprisonment by "the power of demons." Later, we are told that "her body shone in the darkness like a precious stone, and her skin emitted sparks" (176). It is as if a dybbuk narrator is playing a game with his readers, giving us obvious historical parallels to distract us from the mythic allusions which convey the depth of his blasphemous vision.

Rechele's initial meeting with her future bridegroom, Itche Mates the Packman, contains multiple references to both historical and mythical analogues. Itche Mates, as was the custom of packmen, examines the mezuzah on Rechele's doorpost:

> [It] was an old one, covered with a white mold. . . . It turned out that the word God had been completely erased, and that the right crown was missing from the letter "s" of the name Shaddai. His hands began to tremble, and he said with sternness, "Who lives here?" . . .
>
> . . . Rechele's long braids were undone, like a witch's, full of feathers and straw. One half of her face was red, as though she had been lying on it, the other half was white. She was barefoot, and wore a torn red dress, through which parts of her body shone. In her left hand she held an earthen pot, in her right a straw whisk with ashes in it. Through her disheveled hair a pair of frantic eyes smiled madly at him. It occurred to Itche Mates that there was more here than met the eye.
>
> "Are you a married woman or a maiden?" . . .
>
> "Nobody wants me!" Rechele said, and limped so close to him

that the female smell of her body overcame him. "Unless Satan will have me!"
She burst into sharp laughter which ended in a gasp. Large gleaming tears fell from her eyes. The pot slipped from her hands and broke into shards. Reb Itche Mates sought to reply, but his tongue had become heavy and dry. . . .
"This is from Heaven." (74–76)

This scene contains suggestions of Sarah's witchcraft, her bizarre manner of dress, her madness, and her sexual forwardness. While Sarah announced herself to be the future bride of the messiah, here Rechele presents herself to Itche Mates as a bride of Satan. Sabbatai Sevi, thinking that perhaps, on the strength of her bold declarations, Sarah was "his predestined mate . . . 'sent for her and married her'" (Scholem, *Sabbatai Sevi* 193). Itche Mates, having declared that "this is from Heaven," sends a messenger to Rechele proclaiming, "Forty days before Rechele was born it was decreed in Heaven that this seed, the daughter of Reb Eleazar, was to belong to Itche Mates" (78).

Intertwined with these historical allusions are multiple suggestions of the mythic. The two sides of Rechele's face suggest the double aspect of the *Shekhinah* who, while usually "the merciful mother of Israel," can also be the "vehicle of the power of punishment and stern judgment." "As the *Zohar* puts it: 'At times the *Shekhinah* tastes the other, bitter side, and then her face is dark'" (Scholem, *On the Kabbalah* 107). Rechele's shining body alludes to the nature of the *Shekhinah* as divine light scattered among the husks. And, in an almost mocking suggestion of the "breaking of the vessels," Rechele's earthen pot slips and breaks into shards.

Furthermore, the powerfully protective names of God and Shaddai (another name for the Almighty), traditionally inscribed on the mezuzah and believed to drive off demons, are rendered impotent for Rechele-*Shekhinah*, ensnared as she is in the shards of evil.[20] The emphasis on the letter *s*, *shin*, in Shaddai, gives hints as to the nature of the evil which awaits her. It alludes both to Sabbatai and to Satan. While Sabbatai identified himself mystically with the name Shaddai, David Habillo, a famous seventeenth-century Kabbalist, associated Sabbatai with "the 'Satan of Holiness' who was mystically indicated by the [four-crowned] letter *shin*" (Scholem, *Sabbatai Sevi* 173).[21] Sabbatai Sevi, the false messiah, ultimately becomes totally identified with the evil against which he sought to fight. Instead of "raising up" the sacred sparks of the *Shekhinah*, he himself is given over to the powers of darkness. Rechele is his victim.

Bride of Itche Mates the Packman, Rechele later becomes mistress of Reb Gedaliya, the ritual slaughterer who comes to Goray from Zamość. These two figures serve to illustrate two aspects of Sabbatai Sevi's troubled personality. It seems that he suffered from an extreme form of manic-depressive psychosis, alternating periods of complete apathy with periods of exaltation, which his followers referred to as "illuminations." During his periods of "illumination," Sabbatai made bizarre declarations and performed blasphemous acts such as shifting dates for the Sabbath and holy days, dressing a large fish as a child and putting it into a cradle, and performing a marriage of sorts between himself and the Torah. Apart from these uncontrollable periods, he was an ascetic who suffered from remorse over his impious acts and, until named the messiah, was unable to understand or rationalize his behavior (Scholem, *Sabbatai Sevi* 126ff.). Thereafter, he declared a new law which reevaluated sin as a holy act and sanctified transgressions as essential to "raising up" divine sparks, thus justifying his own "strange actions" (Scholem, *Sabbatai Sevi* 223).

The joyful licentiousness of Sabbatai's periods of "illumination" characterizes much of the behavior of Reb Gedaliya, while the melancholy piety of his depressive periods is echoed in Itche Mates. Reb Gedaliya enters Goray with the good news of imminent redemption and, like the gentleman from Cracow, slowly undermines the community's traditions of faith. While Sabbatai sanctified transgressions of the law, giving formal ritual blessings to sin, Gedaliya reverses the laws of purity, permitting men to mingle with women and unleavened bread with meat, and, just as Sabbatai did, he calls upon women to read the Torah (Scholem, *Sabbatai Sevi* 403). Sabbatai's sexual excesses became the material for widespread speculation. Scholem writes that his behavior "presents a strange mixture of drives and inhibitions. . . . When he became master over a large number of enthusiastic followers he could indulge his fondness of alternating semierotic and semiascetic rituals." His was an "erotic mysticism" (*Sabbatai Sevi* 880). So too is Reb Gedaliya's. His licentiousness becomes a whispered legend in Goray and is emulated throughout the village. "He demonstrated by means of cabala that all the laws in the Torah and the Shulchan Aruch referred to the commandment to be fruitful and multiply; and that, when the end of days was come, not only would Rabbi Gershom's ban on polygamy become null and void, but all the strict 'Thou shalt nots,' as well" (147).

In contrast, Itche Mates "engaged in a constant round of mortifications" (121), perpetually mumbling prayers, rolling in snow, denying himself sleep. However, he is accused by the Rabbi of Lublin of secretly clinging, despite his asceticism, "to Satan and to Lilith":

This forger and seducer doth give himself out to be a great man, as is the way of all who practice to deceive. He hath made a pit and digged it for young and old, to take them captive through his hypocritical piety and alien ways, the like of which no eye hath ever seen before. . . . To make matters worse, this false prophet is forever sunk in melancholy, whose root is lust. . . . In every town he comes to he speaks upon the heart of some woman to join him in the bond of matrimony, but his purpose is to make her unclean and to give her a bad name. For after marriage his wives all move away from him, because of his ugly ways; from too much magic working, he has himself been caught in the web, and no longer has the strength to act the man's part. (89–91)

Such accusations prove to be reliable. Like Sabbatai, who, dispensing with the law, often encouraged dancing between men and women, Itche Mates leads the townspeople of Goray into the profanation of the ball which Rabbi Benish had sought to stop. Furthermore, when Itche Mates marries Rechele, he fails to consummate the marriage. Instead, he terrifies his bride with his erotic visions:

> All at once he spoke, in a low hoarse voice full of childish mystery:
> "Do you see anything, Rechele?"
> "No! What do you see, Itche Mates?"
> "Lilith!" Reb Itche Mates cried, and it seemed to Rechele that the vision pleased him. "Look at her. Long hair like yours. Naked. Concupiscent." (133)

Sabbatai, too, had a series of unconsummated marriages and was plagued by explicitly sexual nightmares, an account of which, Scholem writes, "clearly describes severe sexual temptations within the conventional kabbalistic imagery of demonic activity." Such temptations, Scholem adds, are typical of those "who embark on the spiritual and ascetic life," but were very disturbing to Sabbatai (*Sabbatai Sevi* 113).

Thus, like Sarah, the bride of Sabbatai Sevi whose marriage was consummated only after a long period of Sabbatai's impotency (Scholem, *Sabbatai Sevi* 413), Rechele marries the impotent Itche Mates, the ascetic version of Sabbatai, but finally consummates her marriage through union with Reb Gedaliya, Sabbatai's sexually licentious counterpart.

The image of Rechele as bride links her not only to Sarah/Rebecca, bride of Sabbatai Sevi, but also to Rachel/Leah, those names associated with the *Shekhinah*, celestial bride of *Ein-Sof*. According to the Lurianic Kabbalah, "Rachel and Leah are two aspects of the *Shekhinah*, the one exiled from God and lamenting, the other in her perpetually repeated reunion with her Lord" (Scholem, *On the Kabbalah* 149). Most frequently, the *Shekhinah* is referred to as "'Rachel,' the celestial bride" (Scholem, *Major Trends* 275), and it is to Rachel, the exiled and lamenting aspect of the *Shekhinah*, that Rechele is linked. "The root of your name is Rachel," Reb Gedaliya tells Rechele, "and Rachel's beauty is yours" (150). This suggestion is made more explicit when Rechele, her skin "semi-transparent," shining, emitting sparks, is approached

by Reb Gedaliya with the words, "Rechele, it is midnight.
The heavens are parting. The Divine Parents are coupling
face to face. Rechele, be of good cheer. This is the hour of
union" (175–76).

When Rechele is imbued with the spirit of prophecy, Reb
Gedaliya again clearly identifies her with the *Shekhinah:*

> The crowd made way for Rechele, as though she were the sacred
> Torah. Some even touched her with their fingertips as she passed
> and bore their fingers to their lips, as when a scroll is taken from
> the Ark. Rechele's left shoe fell and Reb Godel lifted it like some
> holy vessel. Reb Gedaliya placed Rechele on the dais table and
> commanded that candles be lighted in the menorah. Then he ap-
> proached the woman, kissed her forehead, and said in a wavering
> voice, for his throat was full of tears:
> "Rechele, my daughter, be of stout heart! Happy are we, for
> the Divine Presence has returned to us, and happy art thou, for
> she has chosen thee!" (157)

The Divine Presence is the *Shekhinah,* immanence or face of
God. And as Rechele is here identified with the Torah, so too,
in Kabbalic texts, is the *Shekhinah.* As Scholem writes concerning one of the books of the *Zohar:* "The author of the *Tik-
kunim* identifies the *Shekhinah,* God's presence, conceived as
the last of the ten emanations, or *sefiroth,* with the Torah in
its total manifestations, embracing all its meanings and levels
of meaning. Thus he calls the *Shekhinah,* 'the paradise of the
Torah'" (*On the Kabbalah* 58).

Sabbatai Sevi had performed a marriage ceremony between
himself and the Torah. Echoes of that ceremony recur when
he declares himself to be the messiah: "He was 'like a bridegroom coming out of his chamber, the husband of the beloved
Torah.' The Torah was none other than the divine Shekhinah
herself. the symbolism had already been implicit in the mystical marriage to the Torah" (Scholem, *Sabbatai Sevi* 400).
Thus, Sabbatai symbolically marries the celestial bride of
Ein-Sof as, in *Satan in Goray,* his fictional counterparts,
Itche Mates and Reb Gedaliya, marry Rechele, the *Shek-*

hinah's fictional version. But Sabbatai's act, instead of revealing him to be the "Anointed of the God of Jacob, and the Redeemer of Israel" (Scholem, *Sabbatai Sevi* 401), is indicative of his usurpation of the messianic promise. Instead of "raising up" the *Shekhinah*, the false messiah, in the personages of the husbands of Rechele, debases her utterly.

The *Shekhinah*, symbol of the Community of Israel, of the Torah itself, becomes the field of battle in the mythic struggle between God and Satan. Rechele becomes inhabited by the warring voices of the Sacred and the Profane. The Sacred, with the face of the exiled Rabbi Benish, chants from the Passover Haggadah, "I am the Lord! I am He, and no other!", while the Profane cries out, "God has died! The Husk shall reign for ever and ever!" (206).

Once, Rechele was "borne on a gilded chair, and accompanied by the most important people in town. She looked (impossible comparison!) like one of those icons that the gentiles bear in church processions" (183). The "impossible comparison" with the Virgin Mary is yet another sly hint of Rechele's connection with the *Shekhinah*. The figure of Mary was associated with the *Shekhinah* by one of the most important Polish Kabbalists of the seventeenth century (Scholem, *Sabbatai Sevi* 85, note 130). The allusion is deepened, blasphemously, when "Satan [enters] into the body of a daughter of the Jews" (217), and Rechele gives birth to a dybbuk instead of a messiah.

Thus does the demonic always imitate in inverse the sacred. While the Kabbalah's imagery of the sexual union of *Ein-Sof* and his exiled bride expresses the ecstasy of redemptive union, in this malefic inversion of the redemptive possibilities of the Kabbalah, the *Shekhinah*, in *Satan in Goray*, is not reunited with her God, but is instead subjugated by a macabre eruption of evil.

Instead of a promised messiah who, disguising good as evil could descend into the *kelippot* to free the *Shekhinah* from her exile, evil in *Satan in Goray* is ultimately disguised as good. Masking its nature with biblical cadences, the conclusion of the novel is a demonic account of the events in Goray which raise the malicious Mordecai Joseph, enemy of Rabbi Benish, to the status of sacred hero.

Rabbi Benish functioned in part 1 of the novel as Rechele functions in part 2. Each is intricately connected with the idea of community. Benish is rabbi, creator of community, and human counterpart of his creator God. Rechele is Community incarnate, shadow of the *Shekhinah*, immanence or face of God. Benish engages in a war against "the others"; Rechele becomes the battleground for debates between the Sacred and the Profane. The one early hint of their parallel stature in the novel, as well as their parallel fates, occurs when Benish lies comatose in his study after his failed attempt to stop the ball—the ball which is Rechele's betrothal feast. The scene switches to the festivities where Rechele, too, lies unconscious, "her hair wild and her teeth clenched" (108). Rabbi Benish is routed by demons; Rechele is raped by them—the earthly counterparts of both God and his *Shekhinah* are conquered by evil. Satan is indeed triumphant in Goray.

Thus, while community, as a microcosm of divine creation, might serve to ameliorate human exile, becoming a source of meaning in human life which could stay the forces of darkness, it is a possibility which continually goes unrealized. Stories such as "The Gentleman from Cracow" or Singer's series of historical novels, which stretch from the mid-nineteenth century to a time past the Nazi Holocaust, delineate not the prophetic fulfillment but rather the dissolution of community. *Satan in Goray* prefigures this dissolution. Here the mythic struggle between creation and the demonic first leads its rabbi into retreat and then perforates the cosmic sanction of the community, propelling humankind into a vision so dark and blasphemous that it seals off irrevocably this possibility for redemption. Such is the malefic significance of Satan's entry into Goray.

5   *Historical and Personal Dimensions of Exile*

Community, Part Two

The forces of evil infiltrate the realistic worlds of Singer's novels much as they do his folktales. Demons still weave in and out of dreams, but they are most evident in the material world, which crumbles under the weight of its own iniquity. The Hell which incessantly intrudes upon the *shtetl* triumphs over the course of modern history: "Evil spirits are playing with us. We came out of Gehenna, but Gehenna followed us to America. Hitler has run after us" (*Enemies* 184).

    The Manor and its sequel, *The Estate*, celebrate the religious community's last knights of faith. In these novels, Singer delineates the gradual decomposition of the Jewish community from the Polish uprisings of 1863 to the last years of the nineteenth century. In the midst of political, philosophical, and technological upheavals of monumental import, a few pious people fervently cleave to the all but shattered faith of their forebears. *The Manor* ends as Calman Jacoby, aware of the dissolution of the world about him and of the hedonism and atheism of his own son, retreats into his homemade synagogue where he chants the first Mishnah:

> Calman did not even remember when he had learned the chant in which he prayed and studied. It had come down to him through generations of ancestors. . . . The Hebrew letters were steeped in holiness, in eternity. They seemed to unite him with the patriarchs. . . . Among these shelves of sacred books, Calman felt protected. Over each volume hovered the soul of its author. In this place, God watched over him. (442)[1]

In a subcelestial world, Calman's faith, hidden within his synagogue, no longer has the efficacy to create a community nor to bind a family together.[2] The murmur of his chant, that sound of God's holy word, diffuses into silence at the conclusion of *The Estate*. There the Rabbi of Marshinov prays for the truth as he dies, and like Rabbi Bainish in "Joy," he finally discovers his hidden God:

> The rabbi thought about darkness. It is nothing but the lack of light, the concealment of His face. . . . Suddenly something fluttered. . . . the rabbi saw a great light . . . [he] closed his eyes, but the light was still there: a radiance that shone neither outside him nor within him, but filled all space, penetrated all being. It was everything together: revelation, surcease from all earthy turmoil, the profoundest joy. . . . He had only one wish left: to let those who had sunk into doubt and suffering know what he had seen. He stretched out his hand to knock on the wall, but his hand made no sound.
> He lingered in this state until sunrise. (372–73)[3]

Here faith, although solitary rather than communal, does exist, and revelations of eternal splendor, although ineluctably yoked with silence, are at least possible.

However, in *The Family Moskat*, the final dissolution of three generations of a Jewish dynasty reveals the collapse of the old world's transcendent promises. Members of the Moskat, Bannet, and Berman families are caught in a transitional era; no longer part of the old world of prescriptive religious beliefs, they struggle with the loss of values which seems inherent in the concomitant rise of the modern world. Singer reveals their dilemma in a series of parallel dichotomies—Hasidism versus the Enlightenment, preservation of faith versus assimilation, *shtetl* versus modern society. Each dichotomy can be reduced to one—that which gives meaning and purpose to life versus that which undermines it.

The disintegration of religious and familial forms of community delineated by *The Family Moskat* defines in small the fragmentation and loss of meaning characteristic of the twentieth century. The novel's family is a metaphor of the human family; its generations, marking the passage of time, reflect the historical process of the coming of the modern world; its disintegrating marriages reflect the fragmentation of the larger human community and the disharmony inherent in a universe devoid of ultimate meaning.

This chaotic, shifting era is mirrored in the novel by a masquerade ball. There, amid a cacophony of shrieks and smells, a surging mob of masked figures portrays the entire world, "Russian generals with epaulets, Polish grandees in elegant caftans, Germans in spiked helmets, rabbis in fur hats, yeshivah students in velvet skullcaps; sidelocks dangling below their ears" (487).

As they do throughout their lives, the guests at the ball struggle for a foothold, lose one another, appear again with someone new or reunite with long-lost friends, only to be herded forward by the throng of partygoers, fragments of masked faces whirling out of sight. Emerging from the crowd, as he does from the crowded foreground of the book itself, is Asa Heshel Bannet—charming, bright, handsome, but sociopathic, a hollow man unable to feel, emotionally crippled by self-doubt and self-hate. As Irving Buchen states it so well: "As a homeless wanderer between heaven and earth and the past and the present, he sums up the terrible freedom of being broken off from God. As an object of inhuman persecution without parallel in history, he begets an unforgettable and perhaps unforgivable source of guilt for all men who in forgetting God have forgotten to be men" (76).

Asa Heshel Bannet becomes an image of the modern person cut off from his traditional religious roots, unable to form communal or personal commitments, bereft of meaning and purpose in a tumultuous world of masked partygoers. He can often be caught glancing into mirrors, astonished at the sight, alienated from a self which is a distant, obscure, object of his own perception. But the hollowness he sees within himself is only a mirror of the emptiness of a universe devoid of all meaning. The final words of the novel pronounce its revelation: "Death is the Messiah. That's the real truth."[4]

Such a pronouncement finds its apotheosis in *Shosha,* which continues the historical sequence initiated by *The Manor.* The various faces of exile which emerge throughout Singer's work all find expression in *Shosha:* the exile of a God who remains silent in the face of human suffering, the exile of the modern person cut off from transcendent meaning, the historical exile of the Diaspora made ever more manifest by the Nazi Holocaust, the personal exile of alienation between one being and another, the inner exile of self-estrangement.

Set just before, during, and after the Nazi Holocaust, *Shosha* reveals an evil so vast that all traces of faith vanish into a holocaustal wasteland. "What can one do? How is one to live?" laments Dora Stolnitz, while the narrator reveals the unspoken answer: "I knew that the world had always been and would always remain as it was now. What the moralists called evil was actually the order of life" (183). In this bleak context, the Kabbalic notion of God's withdrawal during the act of creation reveals its dark implications: "Where is it written that there must be a purpose?" asks Dr. Morris Feitelzohn, the narrator's greatest friend. "Maybe chaos *is* the purpose. You've glanced into the cabala, and you know that before Ain Sof created the world He first dimmed His light and formed a void. It was only in this void that the Emanation commenced. This divine absence may be the very essence of creation" (51).

In this world of evil, made manifest by the absence of God, there exists one being of complete innocence—Shosha, a child-woman, stunted by illness at the age of fifteen and scarcely aged either in body or intellect ever since. She is rediscovered by the narrator, Aaron Greidinger, who had known her twenty years before, and against all logic, he loves and marries her.

More a figment of the narrator's lost childhood than an actual woman, she is his source of inspiration, the nexus of his remembered folk materials.[5] Aaron is a writer who closely resembles Singer in myriad, obvious details ranging from the subjects of the stories he writes to his childhood address and

younger brother's name. Aaron's journey from the sophisticated circles of the Warsaw literati to his childhood home
where he rediscovers Shosha is a symbolic journey both back-
ward in time to a lost spiritual world and inward to the roots of
his own identity.

Twice Aaron attempts to return from this journey with
Shosha, bringing her out into what he calls the "New World."
Once on a carriage ride out of their childhood world of Kroch-
malna Street, she grows too frightened and must return; later,
on the second day after leaving Warsaw, fleeing Nazi persecution, she dies. It is as if one of her innocence cannot survive in
a world of utter evil. In this new world, her innocence itself is
like an illness which stunts her, making her not merely an
anachronism but a mental aberration. "She belongs in an in-
stitution" (81), Aaron is told.

An allegorical figure, Shosha embodies the values and
promises of a lost world which can no longer survive except in
memory or legend. Thus, although Shosha dies, she lives on
in Aaron, that fictional author who, like Singer, survives the
Holocaust to infuse the new world with his childhood vision,
to let that lost world survive amid the chaos and darkness of
the new.

Singer's sequence of historical novels reveals a steady pro-
gression, already prefigured in *Satan in Goray*, from the old
world of transcendent promises to a new world of evil realiza-
tions. Calmon Jacoby and the Rabbi of Marshinov remain a
part of the sacred world of their forebears; Asa Heshel Bannet
survives the transition from old to new but only as a "homeless wanderer" bereft of meaning; Shosha, image of a magical
childhood in the sacred world, dies. In *The Magician of
Lublin,* Yasha Mazur finds himself caught between these two
worlds—the one sacred, the other profane. He vacillates between the two on a journey from exile towards the possibility
of redemption through community.

Tightrope walker and master of illusion, Yasha insouciantly
juggles a wife and three mistresses until, utterly debasing
himself, he uses his mastery of locks to attempt a petty theft.

We follow the magician on a journey from country to city and back again, from a place of innocence to one of experience, from the *shtetl* to Warsaw, from his pious wife Esther to the most sophisticated of his lovers, Emilia, a "high-born professor's widow" (335). During the journey, the complexities of Yasha's life unfold. One by one, the women with whom he entangles his life are introduced and the temptations which beset him increase until, after catastrophic incidents in Warsaw, the journey reverses itself and he loses in quick succession his confidence, his career, and his lovers, returning homeward to his motherly wife in Lublin only to wall himself up in a womb-like penitential cell which, with its one small opening, permits all the evil he now seeks to evade to swarm in one-hundred-fold.

Doubly emphasizing the fragmentation of familial forms of community, the first three chapters of the novel introduce two love triangles, one mirroring, at a much lower social and cultural level, the other. The primary triangle involves Yasha, his wife Esther, and Emilia. The childless Esther mothers the boyishly imaginative magician, keeping his traditional Jewish home, faithfully anticipating his every need, asking no questions about his long absences. The Gentile Emilia, on the other hand, aloof and demanding not only marriage but his conversion, ultimately forces Yasha into making choices central to his whole life.

The secondary triangle involves Yasha, his assistant Magda, and a whore, Zeftel. While living in Warsaw during performances, it is Magda who acts as wife for him. He visits at her home in Piask, acting as the devoted son-in-law to Magda's mother, Elzbieta. Esther's childlessness is displaced into the childlike figure of Magda, while her maternal devotion to Yasha is reflected in Elzbieta who "was like a mother to him" (347), cooking, advising, warning, even interpreting his dreams. Yasha creates a second family with these Polish peasants. And he is as unfaithful to this family as he is to his first. The widowed Emilia's counterpart in this triangle is Zeftel, the deserted wife of a thief, to whom Yasha comes through back alleys and gives three-ruble bills. When she follows him from Piask to Warsaw, her presence leads to Magda's suicide which, like Emilia's demands, propels Yasha into a face-to-face confrontation with his own self.

Despite the sexual intrigue, the novel is only superficially about an amorous magician; in truth, it concerns still another of Singer's exiled meditants, one who, like Harry Bendiner, asks, "What was life's purpose if one did not know why one was born nor why one died?" (410). Like Ozer Mecheles of "On a Wagon," the narrator of "Alone," and other of Singer's characters whose problems appear to be sexual but are really spiritual, Yasha is beset by a weariness explainable not merely by a surfeit of women but by an endlessly questioning mind.

The initial paragraph of the novel makes clear Singer's focus on the spiritual, rather than the sexual, quester. It introduces Yasha in bed but, significantly, reveals not the licentious trickster the reader soon comes to know, but the lonely traveler, overcome by weariness, who has nicknamed his brace of gray mares, Dust and Ashes. Here are the hints—of the wanderer, of weariness, of mortality—which suggest the real nature of Yasha's dilemma. Although always masked by his sexual entanglements, Yasha's search is a search for meaning.

His is a journey of painful self-discovery. The tightrope upon which he performs is an image of his journey through life, juggling and balancing his audience of four women, turning somersaults for them upon the high wire. But it also mirrors the tension of his even more perilous inner journey where demonic imagery serves to reveal the dark reaches of his soul: "He constantly felt that only the thinnest of barriers separated him from those dark ones who swarmed around him, aiding him and thwarting him, playing all sorts of tricks on him. He, Yasha, had to fight them constantly or else fall from the tightrope, lose the power of speech, grow infirm and impotent" (425). Yasha is terrified of the demons which he discovers within himself, fearful of his own capacity for evil and of the possibility of losing the precarious balance he maintains on his inner tightrope, of falling off into a kind of madness, landing smack in the middle of the demonic part of the self.

The fragmentation in his life, evident in his drifting from one woman to another and from one "family" to another, is indicative of a more profound fragmentation within himself. Yasha does not know who he is nor whom he might become: "He was a maze of personalities—religious and heretical, good and evil, false and sincere. He could love many women at once. Here he was, ready to renounce his religion, yet— when he found a torn page from a holy book he always picked it up and put it to his lips" (372).

This master of illusion camouflages himself, adopting protective coloration which blends him into any environment and which effectively hides him from himself. He lives in an eternal present, focusing totally on whomever he is with, promising anything, and not knowing himself "if he were telling the truth or lying" (378). Although throughout his work, Singer maintains that darkness in human life is necessary so that we might have the free will to create ourselves, Yasha is incapable of exercising his will, of making any choice which might create for him the meaning he seeks.[6] He tries "to will a sort of decision, but none would come" (375). Alone on his particular tightrope, "merely inches from disaster" (351), Yasha is in exile from himself.

Yasha's search for self-definition is rendered in terms of a quest for a larger source of meaning, one which, while transcending the self, might also affirm it. It is a search for God. In Singer's work, the exile from self and the exile from one's religious roots are intricately connected, and often, as in "On a Wagon," a religious apotheosis concludes with a revelation not of God, but of self. In The Magician of Lublin, the images of God and of the magician are conflated, so that Yasha's ontological search for self has an especially close counterpart to his spiritual search for God.

The association of God with the magician is a prevalent one in the folklore of the Hasidim. Magicians were the folk equivalent of seers. Knowledgeable about the holy books and the magical possibilities of the Kabbalah, they shared in special ways the powers of illusion attributed to God.[7] "Oh, God Almighty, You are the magician, not I!" (374), whispers Yasha, marveling at the beauty of a summer day, finding his magician-God, like the Kabbalists did, in the miracle of creation. "God is mightier than you, Uncle Yasha," teases Emilia's daughter Halina. "He can perform even finer tricks" (400).

Yasha is but a debased form of the traditional magician. He is a performer, not a prophet, amusing people with his tricks rather than performing miracles. However, like his hidden God, he also "concealed much" (323); his powers, too, are hidden, secret, unknowable. Esther thinks of him in the terms often reserved for God: "She had long since come to the conclusion that she would never be able to understand all his complexities. He possessed hidden powers; he had more secrets than the blessed Rosh Hashonah pomegranate has seeds" (324).

There is a dark side to these images of the God-like magician. Yasha treats people with the same ultimate indifference with which his God is accused of treating humankind. The results of his cruelty reach a climax when his lover Magda hangs herself. When Yasha discovers her, we read: "The stillness of death hung over the apartment, a silence pregnant with strangled screams. . . . Her lips were silent and yet she was screaming—a cry such as no mortal could long endure. Swollen and cracked, the mouth shouted, Look what you have done to me! Look! Look!" (518).

In Yasha's imagination, Magda cries out to him in the same way that so many of Singer's characters cry out to their God. If no mortal can long endure such cries, it would seem that perhaps their hidden God can. Singer has defined the human condition in terms of our exile in a universe silent in the face of human questioning. Here, in the presence of Magda, that definition takes on a macabre intensity. The silence of the universe is not a benign stillness; it is a silence pregnant with the strangled screams of humankind.

If, on his journey toward spiritual and ontological knowledge, Yasha vacillates between sacred and profane worlds, then the sacred is signified by the piety of his wife and by his own religious inclinations, while the profane, consisting of "fragments of a shattered universe" (Eliade 24), is characterized by the swollen and cracked, silent yet screaming mouth of the dead Magda.

Yasha's movement between sacred and profane worlds is defined by the overall pattern of the novel as a journey from *shtetl* to city and back again. In addition, the novel is comprised of a carefully made design of smaller swings between sacred and profane spaces, rendered in sequences which alternate between prayerhouses and public places. Each sequence serves to illuminate the themes of exile and community.[8]

The first of these sequences, moving from a tavern to the threshold of a prayerhouse, contains, in small, the essential elements of the novel—exile, temptation, and the possibility for redemption through community. The first of the novel's public places is Bella's Tavern in Lublin where Yasha, like his God, is the object of doubt; the authenticity of his magic is debated, and Yasha is left to complain that "they see with their own eyes but they don't believe" (328). Just as Yasha is unable to form a faithful community with either of his "families," so too he fails to form community with others in the tavern, although he sits and chats with Schmul the Musician. "Each person has his secrets" (328), he muses, revealing secretiveness itself to be a form of exile, a withholding or hiding of oneself in a relationship—the human counterpart of God's withdrawal, His hiding of His face.

Yasha abandons this profane space and pauses in the darkness at the threshold of a prayerhouse:

> For a moment, Yasha lingered at the open door inhaling the mixture of wax, tallow, and something musty—something which he remembered from childhood. Jews—an entire community of them—spoke to a God no one saw. . . . Though Yasha, like his father and grandfather, had been born here, he remained a stranger—not simply because he had cast off his Jewishness but because he was always a stranger, here and in Warsaw, amongst Jews as well as Gentiles. They were all settled, domesticated—

while he kept moving. They had children and grandchildren; there were none for him. They had their God, their saints, their leaders—he had only doubt. (330)

Outside, in the night, where streetlights "scarcely illumined their own darkness" (330), Yasha is utterly exiled from self, from others, from God, from meaning. He looks into the prayerhouse which, in contrast, is lit up by one memorial candle, and he recognizes his exile from this "long-established community" (329), but he cannot cross the threshold and move through the open door to unite with this community.

"For a believer," Eliade writes,

the church shares in a different space from the street in which it stands. The door that opens on the interior of the church actually signifies a solution of continuity. The threshold that separates the two spaces also indicates the distance between two modes of being, the profane and the religious. The threshold is the limit, the boundary, the frontier that distinguishes and opposes two worlds—and at the same time the paradoxical place where those worlds communicate, where passage from the profane to the sacred world becomes possible. (25)

Such a passage is not yet possible for Yasha. He turns away, and, in the darkness, a vision of Emilia's face, both shy and lustful, looms before him and then retreats, moving backwards "like a holy placard in a religious procession" (331). As this imagery suggests, Emilia, like Bella Felhendler in "On a Wagon" and the Cuban witch of "Alone," presents Yasha with both a sexual and a spiritual temptation. To choose Emilia is to choose conversion and thus to close off forever access to the Jewish community signified by the prayerhouse. However, Emilia and the prayerhouse are not the only choices open to Yasha. Having turned away from the prayerhouse to look upon the face of his temptation, he is suddenly jostled in the darkness by Haskell, the water bearer:

He seemed to have sprung out of the earth. The red beard picked up glints of light from somewhere.
"Haskell, is it you?"
"Who else?"

"Isn't it late to carry water?"
"I need money for the holidays."
Yasha rummaged in his pocket, found a twenty-grochen piece.
"Here, Haskell."
Haskell bristled. "What's this? I don't take alms."
"It's not alms, it's for your boy to buy himself a butter-cookie."
"All right, I'll take it—and thanks."
And Haskell's dirty fingers intertwined for a moment with
Yasha's. (331–32)

Here Yasha is presented with an alternative both to the profane world proffered by Emilia and to the lost sacred world of
his Jewishness. Alone in a darkness unlit by any memorial
candles, that is, exiled in the darkness of a universe devoid of
transcendence, one can intertwine one's fingers with those of
another and through the symbolism of that act form a measure
of community. Human exile can be shared and, in that sharing, overcome.

Such a glimpse of community asserted in the face of darkness finds its profane counterpart in the novel's second public
place. Leaving Lublin, Yasha visits Piask where he dallies
with the whore Zeftel and reunites with a society of thieves.
In contrast to Bella's Tavern, the thieves of Piask form a tightly
knit community which enfolds Yasha. He has known them
since childhood; they tease and challenge and admire him;
and with a gesture of hands which echoes his encounter with
Haskell, the water bearer, they offer him kinship: "Clasp my
hand and join the brotherhood," says Berish Visoker, the card
shark (367).

But this brotherhood, which promises to strew his path
with gold, is not a redemptive communal order which can re-
solve for Yasha his spiritual and ontological quests. To the contrary, it tempts him to forget his search for meaning and, in so
doing, presents him with a temptation even more seductive
than Emilia's.

Central to this scene is the image of Yasha, blindfolded,
opening a complex lock with which Blind Mechl, the lock-
breaker, tests him. This tableau suggests the essence of each

of Singer's meditants—exiled in the darkness, blindly search-
ing for an answer. Opening the lock is analogous to solving
the riddles of the universe. While the traditional magician
probed the mysteries of the cosmos, Yasha probes an elaborate lock with a piece of wire, "penetrating deeper," until the
wire "revealed all the secrets. . . . Complex as it seemed, it
was as childishly simple as the riddles schoolboys ask each
other in cheder" (370–71).

Yasha's symbolic unlocking of self and universe is demeta-
phorized in the profane context of the den of thieves. The
thieves of Piask would rob him of his difficult journey inward,
for they tempt him to profane his talents as a magician for
worldly rather than for spiritual ends, and they offer him an
easy end of exile if only he would embrace the life of a thief
and join the "brotherhood" of Piask.

A synagogue offers Yasha a contrasting vision of brotherhood. On his journey from Piask to Warsaw with Magda,
Yasha takes shelter from a violent storm in the novel's second
sacred space. As he drives at daybreak into a synagogue court-
yard, the sky begins to clear. In the prayerhouse, by the light
of the flickering memorial candle and of the rising sun which
suffuses the room "with a purple glow as if from a heavenly
lamp" (380), Yasha reads the Ten Commandments. He feels
"part of this community. Its roots were his roots" (381), but
he chooses not to pray and instead leaves the prayerhouse,
exiling himself from this community to pose as a Gentile at a
nearby inn.

However, having set forth on a journey of self-discovery,
Yasha cannot escape its inevitable revelations. At the inn, in
the guise of the grandson of the Jewish proprietors, he sees a
vision of himself which cuts through any disguise which he
may assume:

> A side door opened and a boy walked in, wearing a lint-
> covered cap and an unbuttoned dressing-gown from under which
> showed a fringed garment. He had a narrow face and two wide
> side-locks like skeins of flax. . . . Yasha continued eating and
> looked at the boy. "Can I forsake all this?" he asked himself.

"This is mine after all, mine . . . Once I looked exactly like that boy." (382–83)

As if alluding to the temptation proffered by the thieves of Piask, the old grandmother "whispered through her whitish lips and nodded her head as if aware of a truth known only to those not deceived by the vanity of worldly things" (383).

Yasha, whose temptation it is to be deceived by just such vanity—by the sophistication of Emilia and the promise of wealth and acclaim promised by the thieves of Piask—has, on the other hand, in his muddled and often uncomprehending way, committed himself to self-revelation. Thus, in a cafe in Warsaw, the counterpart of Bella's Tavern and the den of thieves, and preface to the novel's third public scene, he sits alone, feeling his exile from those around him:

He, Yasha, was to all appearances their equal, yet a barrier separated them. But what was it? He never found a clear explanation. Together with his ambition and lust for life, dwelt a sadness, a sense of the vanity of everything, a guilt that could never be repaid nor forgotten. What was life's purpose if one did not know why one was born nor why one died? . . . Had he been brought into the world simply to turn a few somersaults and deceive a number of females? . . .
The waiter was at the table.
"What does the gentleman wish?"
"To pay," Yasha said.
His words seemed ambiguous—as if he had intended saying: To pay for my deceitful life. (410)

Immediately the scene changes and Yasha's sexual deceit is magnified and put on stage when, at a theater with Emilia, he watches, in emotional turmoil, a comedy about a licentious tutor who carries on affairs with, among others, a mother and daughter. Yasha sits, forced to face his own lust and guilt and the fears which arise in him when he thinks of Emilia's daughter and wonders whether he is capable of seducing even her. Looking into himself, he sees clearly the choices before him, the choices which will define himself for himself. "He felt the wrangling of the forces within him, the good and the evil"

(414). His choice is clear; it has already been articulated as "between his religion and the cross, between Esther and Emilia, between honesty and crime" (377).

Yasha falls prey to his temptations. He chooses to profane his sacred gifts, to give up his sacred search, to choose the vanity of worldly things—to steal. His object is to crack the safe of a wealthy miser. But his magiclike powers desert him and in their place he feels an ominous presence, "a dybbuk, a satan, an implacable adversary who would disconcert him while he was juggling, push him from the tightrope, make him impotent" (456). He fails in his attempt to steal and, in fleeing, injures his leg. He takes shelter in the third of the novel's sacred spaces.

Here Yasha undergoes an emotional transformation which, in moving him from his exile into a redemptive community, mirrors in small the thrust of his entire journey. He enters a prayerhouse on Gnoyne Street, in flight from the police; he is in hiding—a state which, we understand from Singer's imagery of the hidden God, is in and of itself one of exile. In addition, he has utterly debased himself through an action which is a betrayal of himself as magician and as spiritual quester. Thus, alienated from himself, fearful of discovery, and suffering great pain, Yasha projects hostility towards himself onto the prayerful Jews, imagining that "the entire assemblage was giggling behind his back." Even one of the fringes of a prayer shawl "lash[es] him across the eye" (463).

But as exiled as he is from the congregation, he still feels drawn to it. To Yasha, it all seems "strangely alien yet strangely familiar" (462). The simple words of a young man reaching out with concern to him breaks through Yasha's exile, enveloping him with the redemptive love of this community and leading him to an emotional affirmation of God:

Yasha distinctly sensed the love which flowed from their persons to him. They are Jews, my brethren, he said to himself. . . . he had betrayed this fraternity, befouled it, stood ready to cast it aside. . . . How could I have forgotten this? How?

The circle of Jews had dispersed and Yasha stood alone in the
prayer shawl and phylacteries, prayer book in hand. . . .
Oddly enough he now believed these words: God had created
the world. (465)

The scene continues with an extended expression of belief,
concluding with his declaration: "I must be a Jew! . . . A Jew
like all the others!" (467).

However, once outside the prayerhouse, on the street, the
novel's fourth profane space, Yasha's religious fervor cannot
sustain itself; it begins to cool and his doubt returns. Like Job,
he raises "his eyes toward the pallid sky. 'If You want me to
serve you, Oh God, reveal Yourself, perform a miracle, let
Your voice be heard, give me some sign'" (469). Whereupon
Yasha sees a cripple:

He was a small man and his head, cocked to one side, appeared
to be trying to tear itself loose from his neck. So also with his
gnarled hands—they seemed about to crack from his wrists even
while he was collecting alms. Apparently his legs had only one
goal: to grow more twisted. His beard had the same contorted
look and was in the act of tearing itself from his chin. Each finger
was bent in a different direction, plucking, it seemed, an unseen
fruit from an unseen tree. He moved in an unearthly jig, one foot
in front of him, the other scraping and shuffling behind. A twisted
tongue trailed from his twisted mouth, issuing between twisted
teeth. Yasha took out a silver coin and sought to place it in the
beggar's hand but found himself hampered by the odd contor-
tions of the man. Another magician! he thought, and felt a revulsion, an urge to flee. He wished to throw the coin to the other as
quickly as possible, but the cripple, apparently, had his own
game—pushing closer, he sought to touch Yasha, like a leper determined to infect someone with his leprosy. Fiery sparks again
flashed before Yasha's eyes, as if they were constantly present and
only needed the opportunity to reveal themselves. He cast the
coin at the beggar's feet. He wanted to run but his own feet began
to tremble and twitch as if imitating the cripple's. (469–70)

Yasha does not recognize this troubling, cruel vision as any
kind of revelation. But if his magician-God is not revealing

Himself to Yasha, certainly He is revealing Yasha to Yasha. And it is a revelation from which the magician flees in revulsion. His flight takes him on a surreal voyage, spiraling downward in loss and degradation, like the cripple "still spinning and twisting as if seeking to bore his head into an invisible wall" (472).

Upon confessing his crime to Emilia, he suffers the loss of her love. Mirroring that loss, the vision of community which he had found in the Gnoyne Street prayerhouse evaporates upon his return there. In this, his fourth entry into a sacred space, Yasha finds that "although it was a hot day, a chill which the sun could not dissipate came from the synagogue" (509).

Returning home, he finds Magda hanging from the ceiling, all of their animals dead, and he flees again through the city as if reviewing the geography of the profane world. Wandering first into a tavern, Yasha sits opposite a giant whose "watery, crossed eyes rolled in exaltation, the ecstasy of one on the brink of madness" (526). Like the twirling, spinning cripple, the giant presents in himself a mirror for Yasha's introspection, and again he flees.

No longer able to recreate the community he once felt in the Gnoyne Street prayerhouse, horrified and humiliated by the glimpses he is given of himself in the faces of the cripple and the giant, Yasha finds himself utterly alienated from the rabble of the profane world whose reality cannot touch his:

> Men shouted, women laughed. No one among all these people knew that someone called Magda had hanged herself, nor that a magician from Lublin was racked by pain. The laughter and carousing will go on until they too turn to dust, Yasha said to himself. It seemed odd to him now that he had devoted his every waking thought to entertaining this rabble. What was I after? To have these dancers upon graves spare me some of their applause? Was that why I became a thief and murderer? (528)

His final loss involves Zeftel whom he discovers in bed with a white slaver from whom she had looked to Yasha for protection:

Now a shame he had never felt before came over him—a shame not for the couple but for himself, the humiliation of one who realizes that despite all his wisdom and experience, he has remained a fool. . . . He felt sorrow, emptiness, a sense of powerlessness. It was not unlike the feeling he had experienced a few hours earlier when he had discovered Magda dead. Twice in one day there had been unveiled to him things which are best concealed. He had looked on the faces of death and lechery and had seen that they were the same. And even as he stood there staring, he knew that he was undergoing some sort of transformation, that he would never again be the Yasha he had been. The last twenty-four hours were unlike any previous day he had experienced. They summed up all his previous existence, and in summing it up had put a seal upon it. He had seen the hand of God. He had reached the end of the road. (533–34)

Yasha's journey out into the world and inward to the deep reaches of the soul has horrified him, and he retreats, returning to Lublin to wall himself up in the novel's fifth and final prayerhouse—a tiny, doorless, brick penitential cell. Having come to "the end of the road," his voyage of discovery over, he both regresses and remains as one dead: "It was as if he had become again a foetus in his mother's womb"; "often he had felt that he was already in his grave" (540).

In his penitential cell, Yasha solidifies his exile. While once he felt his alienation as a barrier which separated him from all others, now he has erected brick walls to keep the world at bay. He thinks that he has embraced his religion and redeemed himself, but he has merely redefined and ossified his isolation.

Yasha's cell does not reach heavenward. Sacred spaces should offer possibilities for transcendence of the profane world, Eliade writes. *"Images of an opening"* express these transcendent possibilities: "in the sacred enclosure . . . there must be a door to the world above, by which the gods can descend to earth and man can symbolically ascend to heaven" (26). Instead of opening up a space through which Yasha might communicate with heaven, his cell lets in the profane world.

From its one small opening comes not the "purple glow as if from a heavenly lamp" (380) but "evil talk, slander, wrath, and false flattery" (546).

Walled up in his solitary cell, Yasha fails to create a loving community which might become a source of redemption for him. His wife Esther faithfully ministers to his every need, but she remains, as she always has, closed out of his life. Like a magnet, he draws multitudes to his doorless room, but rather than forming a new community, these people wail and shriek, demand and plead, pounding upon his one shuttered window:

> A deserted wife, whose husband had been missing six years and who had been searching throughout Poland for him, screamed so loudly that Yasha had to stuff his ears. She hurled herself at the building as if determined, from sheer bitterness, to demolish the structure. Her breath stank of onions and rotting teeth. Those standing behind her on line demanded that she make her complaints briefer, but she waved her fists at them and continued shouting and wailing. Finally, she was dragged away. "Scum, whoremaster, murderer!" she shouted at Yasha. (548)

The magician's failure to create a truly sacred space, one which, transcending the profane world, might reach heavenward, is not simply a personal failure. Singer repeatedly makes clear that it is the condition of humankind to be exiled in a universe devoid of the possibility of such transcendence.[9] But through the image of Haskell, the water bearer, Singer has indicated an alternative to our exile. By intertwining our fingers with those of another, we can form human community, and, in so doing, although perhaps only momentarily and provisionally, we can begin to transcend our exile through the act of sharing it. Yasha fails to recognize that such possibilities for redemption have always been his.

6   *Redemption*

In Singer's memoirs of his childhood, *In My Father's Court*, is a story called "Old Jewishness" which ends with a young man on the threshold of a synagogue lamenting the death of his father: "'Oh Father, Father, why did you leave us?' he cried" (290). The Christian echo of this lament is *"Eli, Eli, lema sabachthani?"* These cries of anguish are essentially neither Jewish nor Christian; they are human. As they question an abandonment which cannot be eased, they awaken us fully to an exile which is the fundamental given of human existence.

The exile of humankind from God and of God from the world is the primary issue in Singer's fiction. While God is a concern everywhere, he is present nowhere. Singer's characters define their lives in terms of their relationship to a God who perpetually recedes from their grasp. But we have seen that although their cries are couched in religious terms, as his characters incessantly search out their elusive God, Singer evokes a universe akin to that of modern secular absurdists, a place where humankind is exiled from any source of meaning and where the phenomenal world forever disintegrates about us.

The hidden face of God is Singer's central metaphor for a universe which remains unresponsive to the human need for meaning. God's absence, the dimming or withdrawal of divine light, is the darkness or blindness of the human condition. To see with clarity, to understand the nature and purpose of human life, is to be redeemed from such blindness.

When the saintly Rabbi of Marshinov lies dying, he thinks about darkness:

It is nothing but the lack of light, the concealment of His face. . . . Suddenly something fluttered. . . . the rabbi saw a great light. . . . It illuminated every beam of the ceiling, every corner of the room, the windowpanes, the bed cover. "And God said, 'Let there be light.'" "And God saw that it was good." The rabbi was witnessing Creation. Within one moment everything had become clear, all questions had been answered. The rabbi closed his eyes, but the light was still there: a radiance that shone neither outside him nor within him, but filled all space, penetrated all being. It was everything together: revelation, surcease from all earthly turmoil, the profoundest joy. (*Estate* 372–73)

Here is a vision of the fullness of redemption. The darkness of God's absence, i.e., the "blindness" of the human condition, is transformed by the light of God's presence in creation. Through the emanating light and logos of the divine, the rabbi "sees" with a clarity which can answer all questions. The divine light is made fully manifest; it is neither dimmed nor withdrawn. Its radiance fills all space, encompassing the rabbi. His exile from meaning is over. To see the face of God is a metaphor expressing the acquisition of ultimate knowledge. But to see the face of God, the Bible relates, is to die. And so the Rabbi of Marshinov "merge[s] with eternity" (373), never fulfilling his last wish which is to share his vision with others.

The Rabbi of Marshinov is an ideal and an exception in Singer's world. The Kabbalic myths which Singer uses to express his vision reveal that with the retreat of *Ein-Sof* in the act of creation, humankind finds itself exiled from any ultimate source of light and logos and is enmeshed instead in darkness and silence. In place of saintly visionaries, we are given wandering meditants who yearn for, but are exiled from, any significance beyond the mortal.

Those who can believe in a source of transcendence do so only, like Gimpel the Fool or Rabbi Nechemia of "Something Is There," by blindly suspending their disbelief and, perhaps foolishly, leaping over an abyss. Rabbi Nechemia rebels against a God who never shows his face: "You want to conceal your face? . . . So be it. You conceal your face and I will conceal mine." The Kabbalists, for whom existence implied a creator, saw the periodic reappearance of the moon as a reminder of the end of God's cosmic exile (Scholem, *On the Kabbalah* 146–53). Thus when Rabbi Nechemia lies dying, creation, concretized in the "pre-dawn moon, jagged and dimmed by fog," inspires his faith, and repeating words spoken to him by an impious but charitable coal dealer, he murmurs, "Something is there" (*Kafka* 286, 311). But while Rabbi Nechemia, in his yearning to find his concealed God, may look at the moon and affirm his faith, Herman Broder in *Enemies, A Love Story* sees in the moon only "the head of a skeleton" (114). For every statement of belief as articulated by Rabbi Nechemia, we find in Singer's fiction counterstatements of profound disbelief.

But the Kabbalah also describes a redemptive process wherein, by creating a sacred community, humankind might reverse the process of cosmic exile and mystically unite itself with the divine. This redemptive process is allegorized as the reunion of the *Shekhinah*, celestial bride of *Ein-Sof* and Community of Israel, with her husband. However, throughout Singer's work, this possibility for redemption confronts again and again the reality of exile. In stories such as "The Gentleman from Cracow" and in his series of historical novels, Singer reveals the dissolution rather than the redemptive fulfillment of community. In *Satan in Goray*, which prefigures such dissolution, he reverses the Kabbalic symbolism of the redemptive union of the *Shekhinah* with *Ein-Sof* and instead shows her utterly subjugated by darkness. Thus, the possibility that humankind might redeem itself from exile by creating a sacred community in the midst of a profane world is a possibility which continually goes unrealized. Exiled from any meaning which is sanctioned from on high, humankind is left in darkness.

That darkness, conveyed by the Kabbalic image of the disappearance of the moon, is commented upon by Rabbi Bainish of "Joy," another pious man who for a time loses faith in his God:

> The rabbi took up the question of why the moon is obscured on Rosh Hashona. The answer is that on Rosh Hashona one prays for life, and life means free choice, and freedom is Mystery. If one knew the truth how could there be freedom? If hell and paradise were in the middle of the market place, everyone would be a saint. Of all the blessings bestowed on man, the greatest lies in the fact that God's face is forever hidden from him. (*Gimpel* 131)

The obscured moon or the hidden face of God, i.e., the darkness which defines human exile from meaning, is, Singer continually maintains, a necessary constituent of our humanity. Without darkness, there would be no need for the freedom through which we can create for ourselves the meaning we seek.

Fiction has the power of revelation. And Singer's fiction reveals to us that despite our exile from transcendent forms of meaning, we are given some form of an answer to the dilemma of human existence. We are offered the freedom to choose the profound consolation of love. Through the image of Haskell, the water bearer, Singer has indicated an alternative to our exile. By choosing to intertwine our fingers with those of another we can in a sense share our exile, and through the very act of that sharing, we can begin to transcend it.

Such is the nature of redemption in Singer's fiction. It is not a messianic event which can restore the cosmos to its intended harmony before God seemed to retreat from it. Nor is it a revelation which can finally subdue that "wild longing for clarity whose call," Camus says, "echoes in the human heart" ("Absurd Reasoning" 16). But it is a redemption from utter meaninglessness for it imparts to life some value and significance. Singer's use of love as that which ends our human exile, if only momentarily and provisionally, mirrors the Kabbalah's

emphasis on sexuality and its portrayal of redemption as the
ultimate union of God and the *Shekhinah*, his bride, exiled
from him during the act of creation.

Yasha Mazur's failure in *The Magician of Lublin* to form a
redemptive human community, despite his many love relationships, is matched by that of his twentieth century proto-
type, Herman Broder of *Enemies, A Love Story*. Herman sees
the whole universe as seething with sexuality: "In the beginning was lust. The godly, as well as the human, principle is
desire. Gravity, light, magnetism, thought may be aspects of
the same universal longing. Suffering, emptiness, darkness
are nothing more than interruptions of a cosmic orgasm that
grows forever in intensity" (48). Such hints of the Kabbalic
imagery of cosmic sexuality are used ironically throughout the
novel, for there is no redemptive love for Herman. Every
human contact was a potential danger to him, and even sex
serves only to underscore his exile from all of humanity.
"You're a stranger" (275), his lover tells him at the end of their
affair.

Herman Broder, "without belief in himself or in the human
race; a fatalistic hedonist who lived in presuicidal gloom" (30),
is Singer's supreme example of a sexuality profaned by se-
crecy, anxiety, and guilt. He is a ghostwriter for a New York
rabbi, a polygamist possessed by the nightmare of discovery, a
nightmare intensified by the memories of years spent hidden
from the Nazis in a hayloft. The specter of Nazi atrocities
broods even over his lovemaking: "The kissing, the fondling,
the passionate love-making was always accompanied by stories
from the ghettos, the camps" (45).

A vivid memory recalled by his lover's mother becomes em-
blematic of Herman's life:

That very moment, as she stood at the stove, she had seen in her
mind's eye a young Jewish girl stripped naked and balancing on a
log over a pit of excrement. All around her stood groups of Germans, Ukrainians, Lithuanians, taking bets on how long she
would be able to stand there. They shouted insults at her and at

the Jews; half drunk, they watched until this eighteen-year-old beauty, this daughter of rabbis and esteemed Jews, slipped and fell into offal. (49–50)

The erotic potential of this scene is displaced into a group act of sadism and of lust for humiliation rather than for sex. The girl falls into offal and it is the offal of the desexed and desecrated humanity around her. Linking himself forever to the scene, Herman says, much later in the novel, "I am sunk in offal and I am myself offal" (270).

Left in a world where redemption and transcendence are devoid of all meaning, Herman can only acknowledge that every lover is an enemy, every relationship is exploitative. He finds only evil in the hidden face of God: "Wasn't it possible that a Hitler presided on high and inflicted suffering on imprisoned souls?" (53). No light of revelation breaches the presuicidal gloom of Herman's existence. We find only glaring light bulbs in cheap casinos against which moths singe themselves and fall dead. Herman's final act is to buy light bulbs for his darkened apartment, around which he gropes in search of a socket.

Like the magician of Lublin, Herman is self-exiled from humanity, alone in a populous world. Unable to form any permanent relationships, incapable of understanding themselves or of the nature of their longing for communion with others, they hide. Yasha walls himself up in a womblike penitential cell; Herman disappears, probably to conceal himself in the perpetual hideaway from which he never really escaped, "an American version of his Polish hayloft" (280).

Like Yasha Mazur and Herman Broder, Dr. Yaretzky of "The Shadow of a Crib" flees from any commitment in a world which he sees as full of suffering and devoid of purpose. "He spat at the sky but the spittle landed on his own knee" (Spinoza 84). One night, wandering about in the dark, he comes upon the lighted window of the rabbi's study: "Dr. Yaretzky stood there, unable to move. He was convinced that he witnessed a love-scene, an old, pious, love ritual between husband and wife. She'd roused herself in the middle of the night to tend the coals of the rabbi's samovar. He, the rabbi, did not dare interrupt his holy studies but, aware of her nearness, he offered silent gratitude" (78).

Like the magician of Lublin who stands in darkness looking in upon holy communities, Dr. Yaretzky, exiled in the night, has a vision of community in the homely love between husband and wife. But, like Yasha, he rejects his vision. Years later, after his death, still haunted by the redemptive possibility he had once glimpsed and chosen to renounce, he now haunts the rabbi's study, perpetually hovering in the window, outside, looking in.

In "The Letter Writer," Herman Gombiner, former proofreader at a Hebrew publishing house, slowly contracts his solitary life so that his only human contact comes through the mail. He writes to women, selecting those who live far away in order to avoid meetings. But when one of his correspondents comes to him, nursing him through a serious illness, he tells her that he wants her to remain with him. Unlike Yasha, Dr. Yaretzky and Herman Broder, Herman Gombiner accepts his need for another and her need for him. Herman faintly echoes his creator-god, who, as the Kabbalah relates, is also a "letter writer" and who also contracts himself, remaining hidden and exiled from humankind, but who ends his cosmic exile through reunion with his celestial bride. This story ends with the familiar imagery of a bride, half-obscured letters on old books, and the emerging light of revelation:

"That is what I wanted to hear." She stood up quickly and turned away. She walked toward the bathroom, embarrassed as a young Kalomin bride. She remained standing in the doorway with her back toward him, her head bowed, revealing the small nape of her neck, her uncombed hair.

Through the window a gray light was beginning to appear. . . . The night had ended like a dream and was followed by an obscure reality, self-absorbed, sunk in the perpetual mystery of being. . . . The windowpanes became rosy—a sign that in the east the sky was not entirely overcast. The books were momentarily bathed in a purplish light, illuminating the old bindings and the last remnants of gold-engraved and half-legible titles. It all had the quality of a revelation. (*Seance* 276)

"The Spinoza of Market Street" also involves a solitary man who finds human love late in life. The learned Dr. Fischelson, elderly student of Spinoza, finds comfort from his loneliness in the thought that he is a part of the cosmos:

Dr. Fischelson experienced the *Amor Dei Intellectualis* which is, according to the philosopher of Amsterdam, the highest perfection of the mind. Dr. Fischelson breathed deeply, lifted his head as high as his stiff collar permitted and actually felt he was whirling in company with the earth, the sun, the stars of the Milky Way, and the infinite host of galaxies known only to infinite thought. His legs became light and weightless and he grasped the window frame with both hands as if afraid he would lose his footing and fly out into eternity. (*Spinoza* 7)

However, such ecstasy is fully realized only when Dr. Fischelson finds an unlikely bride in a neighboring spinster— tall and lean and black, with a broken nose, a hoarse voice, and a mustache on her upper lip. Only in moving from an intellectual to a physical love does he truly overcome his exile and merge with the universe.

The radical change which takes place in Dr. Fischelson's life when he embraces Black Dobbe is reflected in the descriptions of the world with which Singer opens and closes the story. Dr. Fischelson, who lives in a garret high above Market Street in Warsaw, must climb even higher to an attic window to look down upon the street or up to the stars. When he looked to the heavens, "he became aware of that infinite extension which is, according to Spinoza, one of God's attributes. It comforted Dr. Fischelson to think that although he was only a weak, puny man, a changing mode of the absolutely infinite Substance, he was nevertheless a part of the cosmos, made of the same matter as the celestial bodies" (7). The marketplace, on the other hand, a "half-lit bedlam," affords him a vision of hell with its screams and shrieks, coarse laughter and savage voices, where knives for cutting watermelon drip with "blood-like juice," and men carry "bundles of wood on their shoulders, reminding Dr. Fischelson of the wicked who are condemned to kindle their own fires in Hell" (7–9). Dr. Fischelson is removed from both these worlds— the heavenly which he studies through a telescope and the hellish which he disdains.

But at the end, after the "miracle" of his love, while Black Dobbe lies snoring in their bed, Dr. Fischelson arises and looks out his attic window, not with his former intellectual curiosity, but with a newfound "wonder." He looks with his naked eye and sees:

> Market Street was asleep, breathing with a deep stillness. The gas lamps were flickering. The black shutters on the stores were fastened with iron bars. A cool breeze was blowing. Dr. Fischelson looked up at the sky. The black arch was thickly sown with stars—there were green, red, yellow, blue stars; there were large ones and small ones, winking and steady ones. There were those that were clustered in dense groups and those that were alone. . . . Worlds were born and died in cosmic upheavals. In the chaos of nebulae, primeval matter was being formed. (25–26)

Dr. Fischelson's vision synthesizes the worlds of the stars and the street. The street, with its flickering light and deep stillness, is described as the heavens had been, while the heavens take on some of the color and chaos characteristic of the marketplace below. He sees the world as one, not two, and accepts himself as part of it—not just part of the "celestial bodies," but of the foolish, physical, human ones as well:

> Yes, the divine substance was extended and had neither beginning nor end; it was absolute, indivisible, eternal, without duration, infinite in its attributes. Its waves and bubbles danced in the universal cauldron, seething with change, following the unbroken chain of causes and effects, and he, Dr. Fischelson, with his unavoidable fate, was part of this. The doctor closed his eyelids and allowed the breeze to cool the sweat on his forehead and stir the hair of his beard. He breathed deeply of the midnight air, supported his shaky hands on the window sill and murmured, "Divine Spinoza, forgive me. I have become a fool." (24)

Human love is also the source of revelation in *The Slave*,
Singer's only novel of redemption. It is set, like *Satan in
Goray*, after the Chmielnicki massacres. *Satan in Goray*, revealing that the possibility for redemption through community was ineffectual, debased the Kabbalic imagery of the
union of *Ein-Sof* and the *Shekhinah*. But *The Slave* uses that
imagery to reveal that only through love and the community
of two it creates is some measure of redemption realizable.

Jacob, enslaved after the massacres, attempts to live by the
tenets of his religion, but he loves a peasant woman. As Herman Broder did, Jacob seeks in the Kabbalah a rationalization
for his feelings: "His investigations of the cabala since his return had uncovered the doctrine that all lust was of divine ori-
gin. . . . Coupling was the universal act underlying everything; Torah, prayer, the Commandments, God's holy names
themselves were mysterious unions of the male and female
principles" (133). The Kabbalic imagery renders belief erotic
and connects the experience of human love with a larger,
transcendent design. Only when Jacob chooses to affirm his
forbidden love does he come to realize that human communion is at the root of meaning. Although his love is in defiance
of his religion, it is only through that love that he finds the
emotional equivalent of his spiritual longing and comes to an
affirmation of both physical existence and a transcendent
source of meaning. "Lead, God, Lead," he says. "It is thy
world" (279).

In "Short Friday," Singer again reaches out for the "true
world" of which Gimpel the Fool spoke. Shmul-Leibele, "half
tailor, half furrier, and a complete pauper" (*Friday* 229), and
his wife, Shoshe, attain perfect fulfillment through their loving faith. The plethora of ritual which they piously enact im-
bues them with a richness of pleasure and love unknown to
most of Singer's characters. Never do they doubt, and not one
demon dares intrude upon their world. When they die, as-
phyxiated by the fumes of their Sabbath stove, they awaken
together in the grave like Poe's Monos and Una. But while
"The Colloquy of Monos and Una" delineates the process of